y as we go on from day to day. But I thank you all. We may not be a...

way as we go on from day to day. But I thank you all. We may not be able to change human

re too near the last war to get it over and to act together. But when the...

are too near the last war to get it over and to act together. But when the time does come when

f Nations, with the World Court, with an instructed public opinion. . . . At least we can

of Nations, with the World Court, with an instructed public opinion. . . . At least we can

splendid thing if the United States could lead the world in a new type of international

a splendid thing if the United States could lead the world in a new type of international

ago at The Hague that it would be possible to hold a disarmament conference, we would have

rs ago at The Hague that it would be possible to hold a disarmament conference, we would have

e a long way from permanent peace. We need education of ourselves; of others; development of

y be a long way from permanent peace. We need education of ourselves; of others; development of

have courage." It would be a great glory if the United States could lead in this new type

en have courage." It would be a great glory if the United States could lead in this new type

C., May 2, 1935

y Celebration, Washington, D.C., May 2, 1935

Jane Addams:

Freedom's Innovator

Letter to the Reader

Dear Reader,

As you read the story of Jane Addams' life, you will notice that unfamiliar words are highlighted with on-page definitions in the margins. This feature allows you to stay involved in the story and add new words to your vocabulary.

Jane Addams celebrated the power of words. Some people tried to silence her for defending the freedom of others or for promoting new ideas. Jane Addams was an innovator—a pioneer—who risked failure and scorn to relieve the suffering of others and to help them enjoy freedom.

Jane Addams tested her words and ideas by putting them into action. As she said it: "I think we all have to feel our way, step by step." The steps she took put her on a path to become the first American woman to win the Nobel Peace Prize.

Whenever possible, this biography uses the words of Jane Addams—or of people who knew her—to capture her life and times. We hope these voices from the past help to bring alive *Jane Addams: Freedom's Innovator*—the story of a woman who believed that all people have a right to be heard.

Deborah A. Parks
Author

Jane Addams:

Freedom's Innovator

Deborah A. Parks

Time Life Education   Alexandria, Virginia

Key Events in Jane Addams' Life		Key Events Around the World
1860 — Laura Jane (Jennie) Addams is born in Cedarville, Illinois.	**1860-1877**	1865 — The U.S. Civil War ends and Abraham Lincoln is assassinated.
1877 — Jane leaves her childhood home to attend Rockford Female Seminary.	**1877-1888**	1886 — A bomb thrown at a labor rally in Chicago's Haymarket Square leads to a riot blamed on anarchist immigrants.
1889 — Jane opens Hull House in the slums of Chicago, Illinois.	**1888-1891**	1890 — The U.S. Army kills 300 Sioux at Wounded Knee, South Dakota, ending the Plains Wars with Native Americans.
1892 — Jane helps to investigate the use of child labor in Chicago's sweatshops.	**1891-1899**	1898 — The Spanish-American War begins. Teddy Roosevelt and his Rough Riders win battles in Cuba.
1909 — Jane joins the board of the newly founded National Association for the Advancement of Colored People (NAACP).	**1899-1912**	1903 — The Wright brothers fly the first gasoline-powered airplane at Kitty Hawk, North Carolina.
1912 — Jane joins the Progressive Party and campaigns for Theodore Roosevelt for president.	**1912-1915**	1914 — World War I begins in Europe with the assassination of the archduke of Austria-Hungary.
1917 — Jane forms the Emergency Peace Federation in an attempt to oppose America's involvement in World War I.	**1915-1918**	1918 — The Allies defeat the Central Powers in World War I.
1919 — Jane tours war-torn Europe and pleads for aid and food for starving Germans. Back home, she is called "the most dangerous woman in America."	**1918-1935**	1929 — The Great Depression begins with the crash of the stock market.

Jane Addams: Freedom's Innovator

Throwing Out the

Garbage

Prologue

1894 - 1898

Drawing of a young immigrant boy in Chicago.

Jane Addams walked carefully through the trash-filled streets of the 19th Ward, a slum on Chicago's West Side. For four years Jane had been complaining about the trash, and for four years city officials had ignored her. The area looked like a dump. Garbage of every description spilled out of huge wooden bins bolted to the pavement. Foul water from backed-up sewers collected in greasy puddles. Alleys reeked of trash smells—rotten fruits and vegetables, the remains of animals slaughtered in butcher shops, and manure from the stables.

The odor nearly made Jane sick. No wonder the 19th Ward had the third highest death rate in the city! By 1894, Jane decided to take matters into her own hands. Fed up with the filth, she began a campaign to clean up the streets herself.

A Deadly Playground

Jane Addams was a wealthy, college-educated young woman and could have lived anywhere she chose. Instead, she moved into one of Chicago's poorest slums. She wanted to turn her home, a battered old mansion called Hull House, into a center where people—especially the thousands of immigrants who lived in the slums—could come for help.

Ever since her arrival in 1889, Jane had watched people die from "filth diseases." In the summer of 1894, the dangers of slum life affected her personally. Her dying sister, who lived in the rolling countryside of northern Illinois, made Jane the guardian of her seven-year-old son, Stanley Linn. A doctor warned that Stanley, who suffered from poor health, might also die if he moved into the 19th Ward. The only things

Ward:

An election district or administrative area for local government.

Photo courtesy of University of Illinois at Chicago, neg. 296.

Chicago children play leapfrog in an alley full of trash.

Immigrants:

People who arrive in a country with the plan to live there permanently.

Filth diseases:

Illnesses caused by germs that thrive in garbage—including typhoid fever, tuberculosis, tetanus, and food poisoning. They are spread by unwashed human hands, by rats and insects, or by contaminated food and water.

Jane Addams with her nephew, Stanley R. Linn, around 1895.

Tenement houses:
Crowded apartment buildings or sets of rooms, usually in poor condition, rented by low-income families and owned by distant landlords.

that could live in garbage, said the doctor, were flies, rats, and disease. "I realized in a panic," wrote Jane, "that my delicate little nephew, for whom I was a guardian, could not be with me . . . at all." Rather than risk Stanley's life, Jane sent him to a boarding school.

Jane thought of Stanley often as she watched other children scramble through streets alongside tenement houses. The garbage bins were their playground. Toddlers learned how to climb on them. Boys hid behind them and threw pieces of rotten food at each other. Young lovers perched on the bins while they talked late into the night. "If the garbage is not properly collected and destroyed," said Jane, "[more than one] tenement-house mother may see her children sicken and die."

Trash Patrol

Jane asked her neighbors for help. Twelve Irish-American mothers volunteered for the job. Forming a "trash patrol," they marched through the alleys and streets, urging people to put garbage in the wooden bins. Their next task was to insist that the city pick it up. The women also encouraged people to wash their hands before eating and to protect their food from disease-carrying flies. They warned mothers to keep their children away from the wooden bins—and the flies and rats that lived there.

Over a two-month period, the trash patrol documented 1,037 violations of the city's health code. The women complained to city hall 700 times that summer. They tried to burn some of the garbage at Hull House, but the smell of burning garbage made the situation worse.

Despite the cleanup campaign, the death rate remained unchanged. In desperation, Jane investigated the private company hired by the city to remove the trash. She found that the owners pocketed most of the money. So, in 1895 Jane submitted a bid to win the trash-removal contract for herself. She was sure that an honest bid would lose. As she explained to a friend:

> *We find that the contractor bid $1000 a month, when it would probably take $1500 a month [to clean up the garbage], then he actually spends about $500. If we bid what it would [take to] clean it [up] we can't get [the contract] . . . if we bid low enough to get [the contract] we probably can't keep it clean— so here we are!*

As Jane expected, the city threw out her bid. Even so, the story made front-page news. After all, it was not every day that a wealthy young woman applied for the job of trash collector. The mayor of Chicago decided to compromise. He appointed Jane as garbage inspector of the 19th Ward, at a salary of $1,000 a year. It was the only paid job that she ever held.

Making the News

After she took the job, Jane found her name in the papers again. One reporter mockingly described the proper uniform for a female garbage inspector:

Some of the Hull House neighbors.

Children in Chicago's 17th Ward play on a garbage bin.

Jane Addams in 1892 at age 32.

Knickerbockers:

Bloomers or loose-fitting trousers, gathered at the knee, worn by women as gymnasium clothes or as undergarments in the late 1800s.

Street commissioner:

An official responsible for the upkeep and repair of city streets.

A horse-drawn wagon hauls Chicago's garbage, around 1900.

How fetching she would look in a trim uniform of cadet gray, with a jaunty military cap set upon her well-poised head, a stunning tailor-made coat liberally adorned with [gold], a proud star on the . . . [lapel], a short skirt and—shall we say?—the daintiest knickerbockers beneath.

Another reporter took Jane's appointment more seriously. "If women accept public office, they must expect to hold it precisely as men hold it." He then added, "Miss Addams understands this."

Jane wasted no time in proving him right. She showed up on the streets at 6:00 each morning to make sure the garbage collectors were on the job. Dressed in a crisp white blouse and a long, flowing skirt, she followed the carts through the streets, either on foot or in a horse-drawn wagon. On most days, Jane followed them all the way to the city dump. If a cart missed a pickup or dropped some garbage, she made the men stop and collect it.

Jane enforced the law. She took landlords to court for failing to provide enough garbage bins. She fined tenants for throwing trash into the alleys. She tracked down the stockyard owner and charged him with using police ambulances to remove dead animals from the streets.

On one street, Jane discovered pavement hidden below 18 inches of trash. She rushed to check the city records. Sure enough, she had uncovered a long-forgotten paved street. After she worked with garbage crews to clear off eight inches of garbage, Jane turned the job over to the street commissioner. When he resisted, Jane fought back. Soon the neighborhood had a new—and clean—paved street.

In less than a year's time, the streets got cleaner, and the death rate in the 19th Ward began to drop. Unfortunately, Jane's garbage-collecting career was cut short by one of the filth diseases—typhoid fever. While she recovered, she hired one of her women friends to finish her three-year contract as garbage inspector.

Dumping Corruption

Jane had never planned to build a career in the garbage business. She took the inspector job to prove that honest public officials could make a difference. She linked the rotten garbage to rotten politics. Jane's nose for corruption led her to one person—Johnny Powers, alderman of the 19th Ward. Johnny Powers handed out the garbage-collecting contracts and had protested the loudest when the mayor gave the inspector's job to Jane.

Johnny Powers was a typical big-city boss. The stocky Irish American was always willing to take a bribe in exchange for his vote. On his salary of three dollars a week, he somehow could afford a fancy house, two saloons, a gambling hall, and diamond jewelry.

Voters in the 19th Ward loved Johnny, however. He stopped evictions, bailed people out of jail, paid for funerals, and gave away turkeys each Christmas. What did it matter if he took a few bribes? As one voter put it: "He has a big Irish heart."

Typhoid fever:

A bacterial disease spread through contaminated food or water that causes diarrhea, vomiting, and high fever.

Photo courtesy of University of Illinois at Chicago, neg. 293.

A police officer arrests a man in the neighborhood near Hull House.

Alderman:

An official of a city government.

Boss:

A person who controls the votes of a political party in an election district.

Jane Addams in 1895 at age 35.

Jane Addams was not charmed by Johnny. She believed he mocked democracy by teaching immigrants that votes could be sold and politicians could be bought. Riding on the success of her garbage campaign, Jane decided to defeat Johnny Powers. In the 1896 and 1898 elections, she threw her support behind candidates who promised to clean up city government.

No matter how hard Jane fought, Johnny Powers fought harder. "I may not be the kind of man the reformers like," he grinned, "but I am what my people like. . . ." Johnny Powers held on to his office until his death in 1913. He eventually replaced the position of garbage inspector with a new job open only to men. But people remembered the image of Jane Addams walking behind garbage carts and fighting big-city politicians.

Jane never forgot the experience, either. She believed that poverty was the greatest threat to democracy, and honesty was its greatest safeguard. For Jane, these ideas were second nature. She had learned them as a little girl from her father. John Addams was a politician so honest that people said "bad men were . . . afraid of him." His ideals had shaped this feisty young woman—who fought poverty and corruption as fiercely as she fought garbage.

Childhood

Memories

Chapter I   1860 - 1877

Key Events in Jane Addams' Life

Key Events Around the World

Laura Jane (Jennie) Addams is born in Cedarville, Illinois.

1860

1861 Confederate troops fire on Fort Sumter, South Carolina, beginning the U.S. Civil War.

Jane's mother dies shortly after the premature birth of her ninth child.

1863

1865 The 13th Amendment to the U.S. Constitution abolishes slavery.

1867 German political philosopher Karl Marx publishes *Das Kapital*, which will become the basis of Communism.

John Addams, Jane's father, marries Anna Haldeman. **1868**

1869 President Andrew Johnson is impeached by the House of Representatives but is acquitted by the Senate.

1870

Elizabeth Cady Stanton and Susan B. Anthony establish the National Woman Suffrage Association.

1872

Susan B. Anthony is arrested for trying to vote in a presidential election.

1875

1880

$\mathcal{J}$ane Addams never forgot the day her father cried. She was only four and a half years old at the time. The sight of two American flags on the front gateposts had sent her racing into the house. Who put the flags there? And why did someone tie black ribbons around the poles?

The mystery deepened when Jane saw her father openly weeping. As she later wrote:

> *To my amazement I found my father in tears, something that I had never seen before, having assumed, as all children do, that grown-up people never cried.*

Through his tears, Jane's father explained that "the greatest man in the world" had died. That man was President Abraham Lincoln, the leader who had guided the nation through the recent Civil War. It was the spring of 1865, and John Addams had just learned of President Lincoln's assassination. "The great war touched children in many ways," Jane recalled. But no part of the war touched her more deeply than the sight of her father's tears.

No Stranger to Tragedy

Jane never knew if her father had cried at her mother's death. She was even younger then—only two years old. What she did remember was standing outside her dying mother's bedroom door and pounding on it with her fist. "Let her come in," said her mother, "she is only a baby." Jane held on to the memory of her mother's words.

Jane "Jennie" Addams in 1864 at age four.

Assassination:
The planned murder of a leader, usually for political reasons.

An engraving showing the 1865 assassination of President Abraham Lincoln.

Sarah Weber Addams, mother
of Jane Addams, in 1861 at age 44.

Jane Addams in 1866 at age six.

Jane's mother—Sarah Weber Addams—died helping someone else. In January 1863, word came that a neighbor was having trouble delivering her baby. With the doctor away on another call, Sarah Addams responded. She knew what it meant to lose a child. She had lost three children of her own. Even though she was carrying a ninth child, Sarah rushed to her neighbor's side. She managed to save both the mother and the baby, but the effort left her exhausted. On the way home, she stumbled and fell. Her baby was born too early and died. A week later, Sarah Addams followed her baby to the grave. Friends and neighbors praised her for having "a heart ever alive to the wants of the poor."

When her mother died, Laura Jane Addams—or Jennie, as people called her—was the baby of the family. She had three older sisters—Mary, Martha, and Sarah Alice, known as Alice—and one older brother, John Weber. Care of the household fell to 17-year-old Mary. Care of little Jennie fell to everyone.

No one took more joy in the task of raising Jennie than her father, John Addams. He delighted in her company, and Jennie adored him. In the years following her mother's death, Jennie would learn many lessons from the man who had taught her that adults can cry.

History and Heroes

Jennie's father loved history. Perhaps it was because his own family had such an interesting past. It was said that his ancestors included some of the original settlers of Pennsylvania, and that one was a soldier in the American Revolution.

John and Sarah Addams continued the family's pioneering tradition. In 1844, they left their home in Kreidersville, Pennsylvania, to build new lives in northern Illinois. Their journey carried them up New York's Hudson River, through the Erie Canal, and across the Great Lakes. Eventually they settled on the banks of Cedar Creek, in what would later become known as Cedarville. Here John Addams built the homestead in which Jennie was born on September 6, 1860.

Jennie listened in awe to her father's stories about the past and about the books he had read as a young man. Jennie wanted to follow in her father's footsteps:

> *I imagined him . . . reading through the entire village library, book after book, beginning with the . . . signers of the Declaration of Independence. Copies of the same books . . . were to be found in the [family] library . . . , and I . . . resolved that I too would read them all. . . .*

John Addams encouraged his daughter to read all she could about history's heroes. Jennie's favorite hero was Abraham Lincoln. "I never heard the great name without a thrill," she exclaimed. Her father had been a representative in the Illinois legislature for 16 years and knew Lincoln personally. She proudly remembered the day her father showed her a thin packet labeled "Mr. Lincoln's Letters." Each letter began, "My dear Double-D'ed Addams." She held her breath in excitement as her father shared his memories of Lincoln and the Civil War.

Homestead:
Land and buildings belonging to a settler.

Wallace Kirkland photo courtesy of University of Illinois at Chicago, neg. 1307.

The house where Jane Addams was born, in Cedarville, Illinois.

Engraving courtesy of Library of Congress, LC-USZ62-60399.

Abraham Lincoln, 16th president of the United States.

The flour and lumber mills owned by John Addams in Cedarville, Illinois.

Underground Railroad:
A network of people and safe houses that helped runaway slaves escape to Canada or to free states in the North.

Quaker:
A member of the Religious Society of Friends, a Christian group opposed to war and slavery.

In Jennie's mind, her father was a hero, too. He believed in ideals such as honesty, independence, and education. She wanted to be just like him. In trying to measure up to her father, Jennie had no idea that she herself would become one of history's great heroes. As a little girl, she just wanted to please the father she adored.

"Moral Concerns of Life"

John Addams taught Jennie what she called the "moral concerns of life." He was one of Cedarville's most respected citizens. He owned a flour mill and a lumber mill and had investments in banking, railroads, and insurance companies. John Addams used his financial success to help others. He built the town's first library, school, and church. He helped to establish the state's Republican Party and, according to legend, opened his house to runaway slaves on the Underground Railroad. A strong Quaker, he believed in peace but stood by President Lincoln when the Civil War erupted.

Jennie wanted to live up to her father's standards, but one day she fell short—she told a small fib. She said her chores were done, when they weren't. That night, Jennie tossed and turned in bed. She tried to sleep, but nightmares kept waking her up. Afraid that she or her father would die before she had time to confess, Jennie crept down the stairs to her father's bedroom. Standing by his bed, she poured out her story. Her father replied that if he "had a little girl who told lies" he was very glad that she "felt too bad to go to sleep afterwards." Telling the truth made Jennie feel "as bold as a lion." She flew back up the stairs to her bed and slept peacefully.

Jennie sometimes felt awkward in public. She was born with a curved spine and had trouble standing straight. Her head tilted to one side, and her toes turned in when she walked. She believed her father must be secretly embarrassed to have such a "homely little girl." But her father proved her wrong. One day when he met Jennie on the main street of town, he lifted his tall silk hat and greeted her with a deep bow. Jennie realized how silly she had been. Her father was proud of her—curved spine and all.

When Jennie was seven years old, her father invited her to join him on a business trip to Freeport, Illinois. They visited a mill in a very poor section of the city. The poverty startled Jennie. She asked her father all kinds of questions. Why were the houses so close together? Why were they so dirty? How could people live this way? Her father explained what it was like to be poor. Then Jennie made a promise:

> I declared with much firmness [that] when I grew up, I . . . [would] have a big house . . . right in the midst of horrid little houses like these.

Jennie's father also helped her to understand the feelings of others. One Sunday, she stood before her father "in a beautiful new cloak, gorgeous beyond anything I had ever worn before." John told his daughter that the cloak was very pretty. Then he asked her to wear her old cloak to church instead. It was just as warm, he said, and it would not make the other little girls feel bad.

John Huy Addams, father of Jane Addams, around 1875.

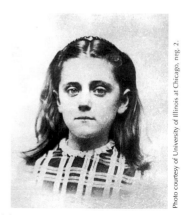

Jane Addams in 1868 at age eight.

Inequality:

An uneven distribution of wealth, social status, or basic human rights; an unfair condition that enables one group of people to have more resources or rights than another.

Jennie was crushed. "I certainly was without the joy of self-sacrifice as I walked soberly through the streets," she later admitted. As they got near the church, Jennie asked her father what could be done about inequality. Recalling his words, she later wrote:

> *[I received] the reply that it might never be righted so far as clothes went, but that people might be equal in things that mattered . . . the affairs of education and religion, for instance.*

He told Jennie that when it came to schools and churches, "it was really very stupid to wear the sort of clothes that made it harder to have equality even there."

Jennie loved talking to her father about important matters. But in 1868, he shared some surprising news—he was getting married again! Eight-year-old Jennie would be sharing her father with Anna Haldeman—a strong-willed, well-educated widow who became Jennie's stepmother.

A New Playmate

The new Mrs. Addams turned the household upside down. She added a bay window and a piano to the parlor. She put white linens and gold-rimmed china on the dinner table. She enjoyed parties and gave them often. Instead of focusing most of his attention on his daughter, John Addams was caught up in a new social whirl.

The piano in the parlor of Jane's birthplace in Cedarville, Illinois.

By this time, Jennie's sister Martha had died of typhoid fever, and her brother and sisters were old enough to leave home. Jennie felt lonely, but not for long. Anna Addams had two children of her own—Harry, a 20-year-old medical student in Germany, and George, a child only six months younger than Jennie. At last, Jennie had a playmate her own age.

Anna Addams wanted no sulking around the house. She told Jennie to ignore her curved spine and play outside like other children. Before long, Jennie was racing around after George. The two children climbed hills and scrambled into dark caves. They picked flowers, collected walnuts, and chased rainbows, searching for the "pot of gold" to be found at the end.

The most exciting places of all were the flour and lumber mills owned by Jennie's father. At the lumber mill, she and George jumped onto logs moving toward the mill's buzzing saw. With hearts pounding, they watched the spinning blade slice into the log. Then, as Jane put it, they hopped off "just in time to escape a sudden and gory death."

The adventures stopped once the children returned home. Anna Addams believed her two ruffians also needed to learn social skills. She held formal dinners where they could practice proper table manners. In the evenings, she read books aloud or played the piano and sang songs with them.

Even though Jennie sometimes resented being told what to do, she learned valuable lessons from her stepmother. Anna Addams taught Jennie the self-confidence and grace that would help her to move from her small town of Cedarville to a bigger world.

One of the mills built by
John Addams, around 1870.

Jane Addams (right) at age 16 with
Anna Haldeman Addams (center) and
George Haldeman (left).

By the time she was 16, Jennie knew that she would soon trade her one-room schoolhouse for a college campus. Both John and Anna Addams believed that women should be educated. As Jennie prepared to set out on her own, she carried her childhood memories with her. These memories, especially the words of her father, would guide her throughout her life.

"To Learn

of

Life"

Chapter 2

1877 - 1888

Key Events in Jane Addams' Life

Key Events Around the World

1875

Jane attends Rockford Female Seminary, later called Rockford College.

1877 U.S. workers in California protest low-paid foreign labor, mostly from China.

1878

Thomas Edison patents the phonograph, recording "Mary Had a Little Lamb" on a tinfoil cylinder.

1880

1881 John Addams dies suddenly of a ruptured appendix. Jane earns a bachelor's degree from Rockford Seminary.

1881 Czar Alexander II of Russia is assassinated, triggering attacks against Jews and forcing many to escape to America.

Jane goes to Europe for almost two years.

1883

1885 In Chicago the Home Insurance Company builds the world's first skyscraper with steel-girder construction.

1886 The Statue of Liberty is dedicated in New York harbor to welcome immigrants to the United States.

Jane returns to London and visits Toynbee Hall, a settlement house.

1888

1890

1895

When it was time for college, Jennie Addams, who now called herself Jane, wanted to strike out on her own. Her two sisters, Mary and Alice, had gone to Rockford Female Seminary, a women's school about 30 miles from Cedarville. Although Rockford was a good school, its graduates received a certificate rather than a college degree.

Jane had set her sights higher. She dreamed of attending Smith, one of the few women's colleges to grant a degree. Not quite 17 years old, Jane had traveled all the way to Massachusetts to take the entrance exam for Smith. She passed the test but failed to win over her father. He wanted his daughter to stay close to home. Jane argued her case, but John Addams refused to budge. Jane finally bowed to his wishes and headed off to "humdrum Rockford."

Rockford College (formerly Rockford Female Seminary) in Rockford, Illinois.

Changing Times

Jane belonged to the first generation of college women in America. The women who went to college in the late 1800s saw themselves as pioneers, and Jane was no exception. She took pride in referring to herself as a "college woman."

When Jane entered Rockford in 1877, the school reflected the ideals of its principal, Anna Peck Sill. Deeply religious, Miss Sill believed women should use their education to promote the Christian faith, either as missionaries or as wives and mothers. However, times were changing, and the women who joined the freshman class of 1877 knew it. As Jane wrote:

Jane Addams in 1878 at age 18.

Missionaries:
Religious workers who travel to a new land, hoping to persuade its inhabitants to accept their beliefs.

The opportunity for our . . . [school] to take [its] place in the new movement of full college education for women filled us with enthusiasm, and it became a driving ambition with the undergraduates to share in this new and glorious undertaking.

Some of the students decided to take extra courses to be ready, as Jane put it, "to receive the bachelor's degree the very first moment . . . the school should secure the right to confer it." Until that day came, however, Miss Sill enforced the same rules and daily schedule that she had followed for nearly 30 years.

Always Something "Doing"

Jane joined a freshman class of 22 students, 17 of whom would graduate. Miss Sill discouraged parents from sending jewelry, expensive clothes, or even food to their daughters. If parents insisted, girls might receive 50¢ a week in spending money, but Miss Sill frowned on the practice. To keep down the cost of tuition and board, each student supplied her own linen and tableware. The young women cooked their own food, washed their own laundry, and tended the wood-burning stoves that heated their rooms.

The day started at 6:30 a.m., with breakfast served promptly at 7:00. Students stood beside their seats in the dining hall until Miss Sill gave the signal to sit down. They were expected to attend morning chapel, weekly prayer meetings, and Sunday worship.

Jane complained about the rules, but she focused on her goal of earning a college degree. She took 15 courses a year, selecting those that would earn her a bachelor's degree at any other women's college. She was

Women's Colleges

Before the Civil War, only a small number of women attended college, and they received the equivalent of today's high-school education. Women's college degree programs began with the founding of colleges such as Vassar, in 1861, and Wellesley (shown above), in 1875.

an excellent student. On a 10-point scale, most of her grades were 9.5 or higher. She even earned a few perfect 10s.

Jane made friends easily and loved to discuss "everything under the sun." Her room became a popular meeting place. As one of her classmates recalled:

> We never speculated as to why we liked to go to her room so that it was always crowded. . . . We just knew there was always something "doing" where she was. . . .

"Doing" included plans to start a science society, a discussion of books, a reform of the school magazine, and talk of learning taxidermy. The school buzzed when Jane stuffed a hawk sent to her by an unknown donor! Most of all, she dreamed of a new future for women. In an 1880 college debate she declared:

> Woman has gained a new confidence in her possibilities, and a fresher hope in her steady progress . . . as young women of the nineteenth century, we gladly claim these privileges, and proudly assert our independence. . . .

The young men who attended nearby Beloit College also liked Jane. She had two suitors who wanted to marry her—Rollin Salisbury and her own stepbrother and former playmate, George Haldeman. Jane captured the heart of yet another Beloit student when he heard her give an impassioned speech. As he later recalled: "She was slight and pale, spirited, and charming. I have to confess that I fell in love with Jane Addams that day and never got over it."

Taxidermy:
The art of stuffing and preserving the pelt or skin of an animal to restore its lifelike form.

Jane Addams, 21, holding a parasol (umbrella) for her Rockford Seminary class photo in 1881.

Valedictorian:

The student earning the top grades in a graduating class.

John Addams and his second wife, Anna Haldeman Addams, in 1868.

Appendix:

A small fingerlike projection from the front end of the large intestine, where the small intestine joins. If the appendix becomes infected, it can burst, infecting the entire body.

The speech that riveted the young Beloit student was Jane's graduation address. She stood before the student body of Rockford and declared: "Womanhood can yet transform the world!" A confident Jane Addams—class president, valedictorian, editor of the school magazine—was ready to face the future. Since she was receiving only a four-year certificate, she planned to enroll at Smith College, earn her bachelor of arts degree, and go on to medical school.

Unexpected Troubles

Jane's plans were changed by a personal tragedy. She was devastated by the unexpected death of her father in August 1881. He had invited her to go with him on a trip to the Great Lakes area, where he planned to invest in some copper mines. John Addams had been the picture of health, climbing hills and hiking over the countryside. Then, as Jane watched, he collapsed in pain on August 17. Within 36 hours, he was dead, the victim of a ruptured appendix.

After a period of grieving for her father, Jane decided to attend the Women's Medical College in Philadelphia, Pennsylvania. She wanted to escape Cedarville and its sad memories. She worked hard at school, but she discovered that she did not really enjoy the study of medicine. Jane wrote, "I am growing more sullen and less sympathetic every day."

Rockford Seminary rescued Jane from medical school. Thanks to the petitions of Jane and her classmates, the school had finally gained the right to grant college degrees. Since Jane had earned more than enough credits for the degree, she returned to Rockford to attend a second graduation ceremony. As she proudly accepted her diploma, Jane was keenly aware of her changed attitude and lack of purpose. "Having a year outside of college walls, . . . I had become much sobered," Jane admitted. "I was absolutely at sea."

To make matters worse, her curved spine was causing severe back pain. In the fall of 1882, Jane decided to do something about her back problems. She asked her stepbrother Harry Haldeman, who was now a skilled surgeon, to operate on her back. She spent nearly six months "bound to a bed," staying with her sister Alice, who was now Harry's wife.

When Harry finally allowed Jane out of bed, he fitted her with a brace to support her spine. The leather-and-whalebone contraption rose so high in the front that it constantly pressed on Jane's lungs. "It pounded and rubbed," said Jane, "but I did not have a backache . . . , so I guess we can call it a success." Jane wore the brace for more than a year.

In April 1883, another tragedy struck the family. Her brother, John Weber, suffered a nervous breakdown, and Jane stepped in to help with his business affairs. She also took charge of her own finances. Her father's death had made Jane a wealthy woman. She had inherited land, stocks, bonds, and other property worth almost $60,000. That was a lot of money in those days—and equal to an even larger sum today.

A Radical Change

Jane decided to put some of her money to good use. In a letter to her Rockford Seminary friend Ellen Gates Starr she declared: "It seems quite essential to . . . my health and temper that I have a radical change."

Jane's sister, Alice Addams, in 1875.

John Weber Addams, Jane's brother.

Homeless people in London in the late 1800s.

On August 23, 1883, Jane boarded a ship bound for England. Her radical change—a grand tour of Europe—would last nearly two years.

Jane's traveling companion was her stepmother, Anna Haldeman Addams. The two women had planned to visit museums, art galleries, and other cultural sights. From the start, however, Jane paid more attention to the people she saw, especially the poor.

One Saturday night, a missionary invited Jane to tour the slums of East London. Nothing had prepared Jane for what she saw. Hundreds of ragged people roamed the filthy streets. Around midnight, a crowd formed around a weekly auction of decaying food—fruits and vegetables too old to sell elsewhere. People desperately bid what little money they had to avoid starvation. Jane would never forget the masses of hands "clutching forward for food which was already unfit to eat." As she later recalled:

> *I have never since been able to see a number of hands held upward, . . . even when . . . they belong to . . . children who wave them in eager response to a teacher's [question], without a certain revival of this memory . . . [and] of the despair and resentment which seized me. . . .*

At the end of her tour, Jane came home more confused than ever. The more she saw of poverty, the more guilty she felt about her own lack of action. Looking back on her two-year tour, she told Ellen: "[I] have gained nothing and improved in nothing."

Jane Addams at 23 during her trip to London in 1883.

A Search for Purpose

The two years following her European tour were the low point of Jane's life. She was bored. She tried to fill the emptiness she felt by writing essays, attending concerts, and visiting museums. The only activity that lifted her spirits was charity work—and she did too little of it. In her journal, Jane wrote the words of a hymn that she felt applied to her: "Weary of myself and sick of asking / What I am and what I ought to be."

Jane hoped to find a purpose for her life by returning to Europe. This time, she traveled with several classmates, including Ellen Gates Starr. The trip snapped Jane out of her depression. By the time she returned home, she had thought of a plan for helping the poor.

Strangely, it was a bullfight in Spain that turned Jane's life around. There she saw the picadors irritating a bull with sharp lances. Suddenly, the enraged bull gored one of the horses with its horns, tossing the rider to the ground. The crowd jumped to its feet and roared. Jane cheered along with them. Her friends were sickened by the blood and left the arena. Jane stayed until the end.

As the excitement wore off, Jane felt guilty. "Greatly to my surprise and horror," she later wrote, "I found that I had seen, with comparative indifference, five bulls and many more horses killed." She was afraid that this same indifference might slip into other areas of her life—that she might stop caring about poverty and cruelty. Jane realized that she was living her life as a spectator. The time had come to stop studying and traveling. She needed to "learn of life from life itself."

Jane's plan was to move into a poor neighborhood and help the people who lived there. She hoped Ellen Starr and other educated women

A bullfight in Spain around the turn of the 20th century.

Photo courtesy of CORBIS/Bettmann.

Picadors:
Horsemen at a bullfight who ride past the bull to enrage it with sharp spears before the matador, or bullfighter, enters the ring.

Indifference:
Having no concern about a situation; not caring.

would join her. Ellen quickly agreed to become a partner in what the two women called "the scheme." For the first time in seven years, Jane felt a sense of purpose. In June 1888, she left her group of travel companions and headed for the missions of East London. Five years had passed since her first visit there.

Lessons in London

This time, Jane did more than tour East London. She actively studied efforts to help the poor. She was especially interested in seeing Toynbee Hall and the People's Palace. At Toynbee Hall, she met a group of 15 well-to-do young men who had chosen to "settle," or make their homes among the poor. They called themselves settlement workers. Toynbee Hall offered help to more than 41,000 men and women.

The People's Palace, which opened in 1887, had facilities that included a large library, a swimming pool, a gymnasium, industrial workshops, and a large meeting hall. In the middle of a slum, people could see great works of art and hear concerts. During the first year alone, more than 1.5 million people had benefited from its programs.

Jane now knew how to put her ideals into action. She would return home and open a settlement house—one of the first to appear in the United States. Filled with confidence, Jane was ready to move into a Chicago slum, "however ill-prepared I might be."

Toynbee Hall

Settlement houses began in the late 19th century in London, England. There, a small group of educated young men tried to help poor people by "settling"—or living—in the city's slums. The first settlement house was called Toynbee Hall (shown above). It was founded in 1886.

Photo courtesy of University of Illinois at Chicago, neg. 848.

An *Innovative* Idea

Chapter 3

Key Events in Jane Addams' Life

Key Events Around the World

1885

Jane Addams and Ellen Gates Starr open Hull House to help poverty-stricken immigrants in Chicago improve their lives.

1889 — Oklahoma is opened to settlers in the famous Oklahoma land rush.

1890

1891 — Sequoia and Yosemite National Parks are established in California through the efforts of John Muir.

Physical education professor James A. Naismith invents basketball as an indoor substitute for baseball.

1895

1900

1905

It didn't take long for Jane Addams and Ellen Gates Starr to shake up Chicago society. The two women moved into a temporary boarding house in January 1889. Within a matter of months, people from all over the city knew their names. After all, it wasn't every day that two well-to-do young women asked people to help them move into a slum!

One wealthy member of a Chicago women's club never forgot the first time she met Jane. "I was hurrying from one committee to another," recalled the woman, "when someone came to walk beside me and began to talk. I paid little attention until I caught the words: 'A place for invalid girls to go and help the poor.'"

"Invalid girls" brought to mind weak, sickly girls taking care of the poor. That idea stopped the woman in her tracks. The sight of Jane startled her even more. As she later wrote: "I turned in my astonishment to face a frail, sensitive girl. She looked anything but the reforming extremist type."

The woman wanted to know more. "Suppose we sit down and talk about it," she said.

Jane poured out her ideas. By "invalid girls" Jane meant young women who were handicapped by too few opportunities to use their college educations. She wanted to find a neighborhood where help was needed and live there herself. She would then recruit other college-educated women to join her. Years later, the woman would say, "You know she had a theory . . . which I still believe is true."

Jane Addams at about age 29, around 1889.

Ellen Gates Starr, Jane's lifelong friend and one of the founders of Hull House.

A rooftop view of a poor Chicago neighborhood, around 1900.

Temperance:
Opposed to the sale or use of alcoholic beverages.

Skeptics:
People who are naturally inclined to doubt. They usually need strong proof in order to accept a claim made by others.

The theory, as Jane explained it, was simple. The nation's first generation of college-educated women needed to do something meaningful with their talents. At the same time, thousands of immigrants struggled "vainly trying to adjust . . . to the life of a large city." Jane reasoned that bringing the two groups together could benefit both.

No Part-Time "Charity Ladies"

Jane and Ellen were a good team. Ellen knew where to look for money, and Jane knew how to talk. For months, that's all she did. She talked to women's clubs, temperance groups, and church-run missions. Some people laughed at her ideas. Others listened politely but made no promises.

One of the skeptics was Dr. Frank W. Gunsaulus, a popular and influential Chicago minister who had seen more than his share of "do-gooders." Doubtful of Jane's intentions, he asked: "[So you want to start] a little training school where young ladies could be instructed on how to deal with the poor?"

Jane and Ellen protested loudly that they had no intention of entertaining part-time "charity ladies." They would live in their settlement house and invite friends from all social classes to join them. Perhaps, they added, the rich and poor could learn from each other.

Dr. Gunsaulus smiled. "Good!" he exclaimed. He told the women to stick to their ideals and he offered his help. Building on this success, Jane enlisted other ministers from around the city. The press began to follow her activities, but reporters often misunderstood her motives. Most of the stories emphasized Jane's "self-sacrificing work" but failed to mention that Jane actually liked what she was doing.

Although the articles annoyed Jane, she knew that press coverage would bring money and moral support for her project. That's exactly what happened. She received offers of help from people she had never met—including students at Wellesley, Vassar, and Smith. In a letter to her sister Alice, Jane wrote: "If we don't succeed after all this help we will deserve to fail."

Missionaries and Anarchists

Confident that she could finance her settlement house—both from donations and from her own money—Jane began to explore Chicago neighborhoods for a place to live. She started with the missions and charitable organizations that were already helping the poor. The Armour Mission, a center backed by the powerful Armour meat-packing company, offered Jane funding if she would locate her settlement house nearby. Jane and Ellen turned the offer down, saying they had little interest in being "swallowed up by a great organization." People at the mission volunteered to guide the two women around the city until they found a suitable place to settle.

Chicago in 1889 teemed with people. The city's population had just passed one million. Only New York City was larger. Nearly three-quarters of Chicago's population had come from other lands. The largest number

A street scene in Chicago's tenement district.

Yiddish:

A language spoken by Jews from eastern Europe; a mixture of German, Hebrew, and Slavic languages, written in the Hebrew alphabet.

Anarchists:

Those who do not support any form of government control.

Harper's Weekly engraving courtesy of Chicago Historical Society, ICHi-03665.

A magazine illustration of a bomb exploding among police officers during the 1886 Haymarket riot in Chicago.

of immigrants came from Germany and Ireland, but people from southern and eastern Europe—called new immigrants—were arriving almost daily.

Jane had hoped her fluent French, German, and Italian would help her talk to people she met in the slums. But she quickly discovered that in the worst areas, where the newest arrivals lived, most of the people spoke Russian, Polish, Yiddish, and Czech. In a letter to her family, she explained that she was in as " 'foreign' [an] atmosphere as I ever felt in Europe."

Jane was intrigued by reports that a group of anarchists were living in the city. In 1886, anarchist labor leaders had spoken to striking workers in Chicago's Haymarket Square. As police moved in to break up the meeting, a bomb exploded, killing seven officers. No one saw who set off the bomb, but eight anarchists were charged and convicted of murder.

Jane had heard about the Haymarket bomb and the riot that followed. She knew that those living outside the slums blamed the rioting on immigrants. Jane decided to meet the anarchists herself.

She found some of them at a "Sunday school" class.

> [A]bout two hundred children [were] assembled in a hall back of a saloon with some young men trying to teach them "free thought without any religion or politics. . . ."

Jane found the affair "quite innocent." She even told a reporter who had accompanied her, "I . . . may take a class." The reporter told her that she had been fooled—these people were dangerous.

The time would come when people would call Jane Addams dangerous. In 1889, however, few people gave much thought to Jane's politics. They simply wondered why she would want to move into one of the most wretched neighborhoods in Chicago.

House of Dreams

Ellen Gates Starr always said that Jane intended to settle on Halsted Street because it would give her a chance to practice her Italian. In May 1889, Jane found an old, battered mansion that won her heart. Jane later recalled it as

> . . . a fine old house standing well back from the street, . . .
> supported by wooden pillars of exceptionally pure . . . design
> and proportion.

The search had taken weeks, and the sight of two well-dressed women prowling Chicago's garbage-strewn West Side puzzled many of the immigrants who lived there. Shaking his head, one old Irishman declared it was "the strangest thing" he had ever seen.

Jane's mansion was sandwiched between a saloon and a funeral home at 335 Halsted Street. A warehouse and offices filled the first floor, tenants rented the second, and a ghost was said to live in the attic.

William Jacobs drawing courtesy of University of Illinois at Chicago, neg. 1291.

A drawing of the courtyard at Hull House.

A portrait of Charles J. Hull in 1876.

Installment plan:
An agreement to pay for something in several smaller payments spread out over time instead of paying the entire amount immediately.

A rocking chair by the fireplace in the Hull House parlor.

The tenants kept the ghost in its place by setting a large pitcher full of water on the attic stairs. Jane assumed this was because "a ghost could not cross running water."

Jane wanted the house—ghost and all. She contacted the owner, Helen Culver, and arranged to rent the entire second floor and one room on the first floor. She also asked about the history of the house. She learned that it had once belonged to a wealthy real-estate investor named Charles Hull. After the Civil War, Hull decided to provide houses for working people and allow them to pay on the installment plan. His ideas were put into practice in Illinois and parts of the South.

When he died, Hull left his fortune and mansion to his cousin Helen Culver, who shared his interest in helping others. Within a year, Helen turned the house over to Jane and Ellen. They named their project Hull House in honor of the family.

Meeting the Neighbors

Jane and Ellen fussed over every detail of their new home—color schemes, decorations, and furniture. Jane spent several thousand dollars—a huge sum of money at the time—fixing up the house. She proudly displayed the family silverware, prized mahogany furniture, and artwork collected in Europe. "Probably no young matron ever placed her own things in her own house with more pleasure . . . ," she later declared.

On September 18, 1889, Jane, Ellen, and a housekeeper named Mary Keyser moved into the house. Friends, relatives, and police were sure that the women would be robbed. On their first night, however, Jane and

Ellen forgot to lock the front door and left a side door wide open. "[We] were much pleased in the morning," said Jane, "to find that we possessed a fine illustration of the honesty and kindliness of our new neighbors." Nothing was stolen.

Burglars broke into the house on only two occasions. Both times, Jane disarmed them, not with force, but with kindness. The first time, she woke up to find a burglar in her bedroom. Other people might have screamed, but Jane thought only of her young nephew, who was sleeping in the next room. "Don't make a sound," she whispered. The startled burglar leaped toward the window. "You'll be hurt if you go out that way," she said softly. "Go down by the stairs and let yourself out." He did.

On another occasion, a burglar ended up telling Jane his life story. When she learned that he was unemployed, Jane told him to come back in the morning so she could help him find work. He returned, and Jane got him a job.

The immigrants who lived near Hull House had never seen anyone like these new neighbors. The mat at the front door read "Welcome," and the women meant it. The motto over the entrance read "May you find hope who enter here." Within three weeks of their arrival, Hull House was a very busy place. As Jane later wrote:

> [I]t seemed understood that we were ready to perform the humblest neighborhood services. We were asked to wash the newborn babies, and to prepare the dead for burial, to nurse the sick, and to "mind the children."

Otto Bacher drawing courtesy of University of Illinois at Chicago, neg. 83.

Artist's portrait of an immigrant family at Hull House in 1892.

Jane treated everyone who lived nearby as neighbors. In return, those neighbors began to trust her. An Italian woman presented Jane and Ellen with a bottle of olives from her hometown. A young man invited them to his wedding. A German woman asked them to watch her baby for the day. In short, Hull House was becoming part of the neighborhood.

Lending a Hand

As Jane and Ellen got to know their neighbors, they began to understand their suffering. They met people who sold their furniture to pay rent, and children who did not go to school because they had no shoes. They could hear old women shriek as they were dragged off to the poorhouse, and young women weep because they could not stay home with their children.

A mother who had lost her child to an accident pleaded with Jane to help her care for her other baby. Because there were no childcare services available, the woman was desperate. "If you could give me wages for tomorrow," she begged, "I would not go to work in the factory at all. I would like to stay at home all day and hold the baby."

Jane refused to allow the misery to overwhelm her. She firmly believed the situation could be improved. The answer was not to provide charity, but to create opportunities for the poor to help themselves. Jane had faith in her neighbors—the woman who shared her breakfast with a family who had no food, the struggling baker who gave bread to hungry children, and the family who took in a friend because he was out of work.

Poorhouse:

Until the mid-20th century, a public institution that housed those who lost their homes because they were unable to pay their debts.

Some of Hull House's neighbors—Italian women and their children.

Jane set a huge task for herself. During the first year at Hull House, she and Ellen started a nursery and a kindergarten. They set up clubs, classes, and lectures. They held receptions, teas, and parties. Ellen established an art gallery.

Barely 29 years old, Jane admitted to her sister Alice: "Of course we are undertaking more than we ourselves can do, that is part of the idea." Jane expected other people—especially young women—to join her in "settling" in the slums. She wasn't disappointed.

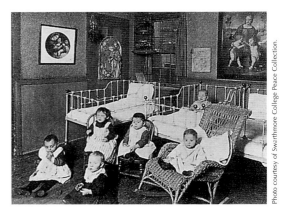

The nursery at Hull House.

Urban Pioneers

People who grew up in the late 1800s sensed that change was coming. The end of the Civil War and the growth of industry had opened the door to new opportunities. The arrival of a new century and the visible signs of new technologies—skyscrapers, electric lights, telephones, and expanding railroads—excited and confused many Americans, especially the young.

Jane sensed the discontent among members of her own generation. She believed that many young people longed to solve the problems of rapid change, if only they knew how. As she said in one speech:

> *Our young people hear in every sermon, learn in their lessons, read in their very fiction, of the great social mal-adjustment, but no way is provided for them to help. They are left in a maze of indecision.*

A drawing of some of the tenement houses behind Hull House.

Visitors to Hull House.

Jane thought the answer could be found in America's sprawling, untamed cities. No other place, she explained, offered such "great opportunities for helpfulness."

The popularity of Hull House strengthened Jane's beliefs. In the first year alone, she had more than 50,000 visitors. The following year, more than 2,000 people a day walked through its doors. Although many came from the slums, others were well-to-do—talented men and women who wanted to be a part of Jane's experiment in living. The most important of these visitors—a core group of women—would soon change Jane Addams from settlement worker to social reformer.

HULL HOUSE

A
" *Nest* of

Radicals "

Chapter 4   1891 - 1899

Key Events in Jane Addams' Life

1890

1891
Jane builds an apartment building near Hull House to help young working women afford places of their own.

1892

1893

1894
Jane's sister Mary Addams Linn dies.

1895
Jane publishes *Hull-House Maps and Papers,* the first organized study of an American working-class neighborhood.

1896

1898
Jane and two other women draft a bill to establish a juvenile court system in Chicago.

1899
Hull House celebrates its first 10 years.

1900

1905

1910

Key Events Around the World

Ellis Island, a new processing center for immigrants, opens in the New York City harbor, near the Statue of Liberty.

George W. G. Ferris designs the first Ferris wheel for the 1893 World's Columbian Exposition in Chicago.

Congress creates the Bureau of Immigration. Lowell Observatory is built in Flagstaff, Arizona.

Wilhelm Roentgen, German physicist, discovers x-rays.

The Supreme Court rules in *Plessy v. Ferguson* that states have the right to provide "separate but equal" facilities for African Americans and other minorities.

Marie Curie discovers the elements polonium and radium and creates the term "radioactivity."

Mary Kenney's temper nearly boiled over as she read the letter from Jane Addams. Jane wanted to meet with Mary to hear about her efforts to organize workers into unions. Mary had little patience with wealthy do-gooders who had never seen the inside of a factory. How could a rich person understand what it meant to work for a living?

The daughter of Irish immigrants, Mary knew how it felt to work long hours in poor conditions for low pay. She had dropped out of school after the fourth grade to help support her sick mother. Although she was four years younger than Jane, Mary already had worked for more than 15 years. While Jane was setting up clubs and art galleries in the slums, Mary was organizing the first women's bookbinding union in Chicago. No, indeed! She wouldn't entertain Jane Addams and her rich friends! "No club people for me!" Mary declared.

Mary's mother had other ideas. After Mary read Jane's letter to her, she advised:

> Sure, Mary, you must go and see the lady. You can't judge without knowing her[,] and she might be different from the other club women. . . . You wouldn't like it if someone you didn't know condemned you.

When Mary arrived at Hull House, she was convinced that she had been right to be angry. She was sure only rich people could live in such a grand house. Then Jane greeted Mary warmly and introduced her to the visitors and residents. She questioned Mary about the labor movement and asked her: "Is there anything I can

Unions:
Organizations for workers to improve pay, working hours, and safety.

Bookbinding:
The art of pulling together the loose printed pages of a book into its cover.

Mary Kenney, labor leader and resident of Hull House.

The grand double parlor on the ground floor of Hull House, around 1915.

do to help your organization?" The question took Mary by surprise. Jane continued, "I would like to help. What can I do?"

Mary tested Jane by saying, "We haven't got a good meeting place."

"The bookbinders can meet here," replied Jane. "Can I help in any other way?"

"Yes," said Mary, "we . . . [need] someone to hand out circulars." Jane not only offered to hand out the circulars herself, she also said she would pay to have them printed.

After the meeting, Mary exclaimed: "When I saw there was someone who cared enough to help us and to help us in our own way, it was like having a whole new world opened up!"

A short time later, Jane invited Mary to live at Hull House. There, Mary attended classes and continued her labor activities, joining a group of strong-willed reformers who pushed Jane in new directions. Jane was beginning to understand that the only way to end poverty was to change society itself.

One Big Family

Hull House had attracted volunteers from the start. Julia Lathrop, an old friend of Jane's, moved into Hull House within a year of its founding. Julia and Jane had met at Rockford College. Julia kept Jane humble by calling her J. A.

One of Hull House's most outspoken residents was Florence Kelley. She arrived one snowy morning in December 1891 and stayed for "seven happy active years."

Julia Lathrop, longtime friend of Jane Addams and one of the Hull House women.

Those seven years were important ones for Hull House. Florence Kelley—a well-educated, independent woman—lived and breathed reform. Florence broke rules. She supported socialism and laughed when people called her a revolutionary. When her marriage to a Polish-Russian doctor ended in divorce, she raised her three children on her own. One of Jane's nephews said of Florence, "[S]he was . . . the finest rough-and-tumble fighter for the good life of others that Hull House ever knew." Jane herself said that Florence "galvanized us all." And it was Florence who caused many people to think that Hull House was a "nest of radicals."

In addition to Florence, the "nest of radicals" included Ellen Starr, Julia Lathrop, Mary Kenney, and Alzina Stevens. Doctor Alice Hamilton led the fight against the filth diseases. Mary Rozet Smith and Louise deKoven Bowen financed many of the Hull House projects.

The Jane Club

To learn more about the hardships of working women, Jane sat in on many of Mary Kenney's union meetings. During a strike at a large shoe factory, Jane learned that the workers who were most likely to give up before the strike ended were the young women who had to pay their own rent. She listened intently when one of them exclaimed: "Wouldn't it be fine if we had a boarding club of our own, and then we could stand by each other in a time like this!"

Florence Kelley, a powerful fighter for the rights of poor people.

Socialism:
An economic system that places strong government controls on the production and distribution of goods and services.

Strike:
The stoppage of all work in a place of business until conditions are improved for the workers. A strike usually is organized by a union.

Hull House Women

Two close friends of Jane Addams who worked at Hull House were Dr. Alice Hamilton (right), who led the fight against filth diseases, and Mary Rozet Smith (left), who helped to finance many Hull House projects.

When the meeting ended, Jane asked Mary to help her with an experiment. She would rent and furnish two large apartments for factory girls. Hull House would pay the first month's rent. After that, the girls would manage and pay for the apartments themselves.

In May 1891, the first 15 girls moved into the apartments. They named their venture the Jane Club in honor of Jane Addams. The experiment was so successful that Jane decided to construct a new building for the club. With funds from a friend, Jane built a red-brick apartment building near Hull House. When a government official inspected the building, he was impressed. He believed it was the first apartment building "founded and managed by women that had ever succeeded in the United States."

Child's Play

One evening, Jane was delivering a speech on run-down tenements and the wealthy landlords who profited from them. Her example was a group of shabby buildings owned by a Mr. William Kent. The guilty landlord happened to be in the audience. He had just inherited the buildings and asked what he could do. When Jane told him to inspect the buildings and make improvements, the embarrassed landlord left in a huff.

Plagued by a guilty conscience, however, Kent showed up at Hull House two weeks later. "I have decided," he told Jane grimly, "to turn over that property to you to use as you please."

Instead of thanking him, Jane replied: "You might tear the buildings down and make . . . lots for the children to play on."

William Kent stalked out, furious that she did not express gratitude for his gift. As he was leaving, Jane called out behind him, "And will you pay the taxes?"

A week later, William Kent returned. "I'll do whatever you say," he told Jane. He later explained, "She was the first person who ever forced me to try to think things out. You may say she converted me; civilized me. . . ."

William Kent's playground opened on May 1, 1892—the first of its kind in Chicago. Young children played on its sandboxes, swings, and giant slide. Teenagers played handball, stickball, and basketball on indoor courts. Local policemen served as umpires.

In 1893, Jane raised enough money to replace the indoor play area with a real gymnasium. By the time the gym opened, however, Jane was involved in yet another project to help children.

Banning Child Labor

In 1892, the Illinois Bureau of Labor Statistics appointed Florence Kelley as a special agent to investigate Chicago's "sweating trade"—the name given to the city's sweatshops.

Florence used her loud and persistent powers of persuasion to involve other Hull House residents in the investigation. She convinced Jane that her efforts would force Illinois to pass a tough new child labor law.

The playground built by William Kent for Hull House neighborhood children.

Children in an exercise class in the Hull House gymnasium.

Sweatshops:

Factories that pay their employees low wages for long hours, usually in bad conditions.

A young girl works at a spinning machine in a textile factory, around 1900.

AFL:
An alliance of trade unions formed in 1886.

A young woman speaks at a labor meeting.

Jane was startled by the number of sweatshops that surrounded Hull House. "The visits we made in the neighborhood constantly discovered women sewing upon sweatshop work," said Jane. She was even more shocked by the number of working children. As she later recalled:

> *I remember a little girl of four who pulled out basting threads hour after hour, sitting on a stool at the feet of her . . . mother, a little bunch of human misery.*

Armed with evidence from the investigations, Jane agreed to campaign for a new factory inspection law. With Florence Kelley and Julia Lathrop, Jane launched a hard-hitting public-speaking tour to " . . . open meetings of trade unions . . . church organizations, and social clubs, literally every evening for three months." Mary Kenney joined them, adding the support of the American Federation of Labor (AFL), which had recruited her to bring women workers into the national organization.

The efforts of the Hull House women and their union supporters paid off. On June 17, 1893, the Factory Act passed by a narrow margin. It banned child labor under the age of 14 and limited women to eight-hour workdays. Illinois governor John P. Altgeld appointed Florence Kelley as the chief factory inspector. She set up an office across the street from Hull House.

Mapping Misery

Spurred on by Julia Lathrop, Jane and her friends continued to investigate living conditions in the surrounding neighborhood. They conducted a block-by-block survey, drawing maps and questioning people about their national origins, jobs, and incomes.

The survey confirmed the widespread poverty in the neighborhood. Most residents earned no more than $5 to $10 a week. Sweatshops and child labor continued in spite of the new law. Parents claimed they needed their children's wages to survive. Everywhere, workers faced dangerous, unsanitary conditions.

In 1895, Jane succeeded in publishing the findings in a book called *Hull-House Maps and Papers*. It was the first organized study of an American working-class neighborhood.

The book earned the praise of experts and scholars, who saw Hull House as a laboratory for social reform. Unfortunately, Jane's book was unable to spark new laws against the social injustices it described.

That same year, the Illinois legislature repealed the Factory Act and closed Florence Kelley's office. These actions were the result of a growing backlash against the labor movement—triggered by violent strikes that upset Jane, as well.

Hostile Camps

Jane Addams had definite ideas about the labor movement. She believed that the rise of big business made unions necessary. As companies combined to form trusts, they made it harder for workers to find other

Outside a butcher shop in the Hull House neighborhood.

Wallace Kirkland photo courtesy of University of Illinois at Chicago, neg. 324.

Repealed:
Stopped or canceled a law or judicial action.

Backlash:
A strong, negative reaction to an action, situation, or idea.

Trusts:
The combining of smaller companies into one large company to create a monopoly—the only company to supply a particular type of goods or services. This practice is illegal today.

An immigrant man and boy in the Hull House neighborhood.

Blacklisted:

Publicly named as a troublemaker, and thus prevented from working in a particular profession.

Capital:

The finances, property, and equipment used to produce goods and services.

Depression:

A sharp decline in the economy that leads to losses of personal savings and investments, the closing of businesses and factories, and the loss of jobs by workers.

jobs. Competing for customers, big businesses drove down costs by keeping wages low and halting factory improvements. A worker who complained about conditions would soon be out of work and was blacklisted.

Jane hated the conflict that was brewing between big business and labor. As she wrote:

> *The organization of society into huge battalions with . . . [trusts] and corporations on the side of capital, and the trades-unions and federations on the side of labor, is to divide the world into two hostile camps. . . .*

Jane refused to choose sides. She wanted to see business and labor work together to solve their common problems. Jane thought that workers—particularly immigrants, women, and children—needed to organize for their own protection. During the economic depression of 1893, Jane watched sweatshop workers teeter on the edge of starvation. With men out of work, women and children accepted lower wages and worked longer hours just to feed their families. To help, Jane opened the doors of Hull House to women trying to form unions. These actions branded Jane as a radical and cost her the financial support of some of her donors.

Economic hardships, worsened by the economic depression, triggered strikes. The most violent strike was led by workers for the Pullman Company, a business that made sleeping cars for the railroads. George Pullman, the owner, had built a well-run company town, complete with libraries, schools, parks, and a gymnasium. He required his workers to live there and pay rents set by the company. When the depression hit, the company slashed wages by as much as 40 percent, but it failed to lower the rents. Workers appealed to George Pullman to raise wages or lower rents, but he refused.

In June 1894, Pullman Company workers went on strike. As a show of support, the railroad union—led by the fiery Eugene V. Debs—joined the strike. Jane urged managers and striking workers to talk with one another, but nobody listened.

In July, family problems pulled Jane away from the strike. She rushed to the bedside of her dying sister, Mary. By the time she returned to Hull House, the strike had worsened. The federal government sent in troops to prevent violence and to force striking railroad workers to let the U.S. Mail trains pass. The presence of the troops sparked fighting, property destruction, and the arrest of Eugene Debs.

Florence Kelley organized a mass rally in support of Debs and the striking workers. The violence left the Pullman workers badly shaken. In the end, George Pullman—backed up by U.S. soldiers—won the strike.

Jane wanted to help the workers, but she had more pressing matters on her mind. She wanted to bring her newly orphaned nephew, Stanley Linn, to live with her at Hull House. Despite the settlement's best efforts, the slum was still a dangerous place to live. The danger had nothing to do with striking workers. It involved the diseases that festered in the garbage-strewn streets. Responding to the danger, Jane embarked on her famous street-cleaning campaign to rid the 19th Ward of garbage.

Jane Addams in 1895 at age 35.

Justice for Kids

While Jane was cleaning up the streets, she also became involved in an effort to clean up the courts. Julia Lathrop asked Jane to join a campaign to improve the treatment of juvenile delinquents. Julia explained that young suspects, no matter what their age, were thrown into prison with hardened criminals prior to trial. Nearly one-third of them were later cleared of all charges. Moreover, first offenders who were convicted of a crime received the same sentence as adults. As one of Julia's friends put it: "Brutal treatment brutalizes, and prepares [youth] for crime."

Jane joined the fight to create a special juvenile court. No such court existed in the United States at the time, but the Hull House women expected Chicago to lead the way. In 1898, three of these women—Jane Addams, Julia Lathrop, and Louise Bowen—joined a committee to draft the bill for a system of juvenile courts. In 1899, the bill passed, but no money was provided to set up and staff the courts. Hull House and the Chicago Women's Club raised more than $100,000. It was no accident that the first juvenile court in the United States opened across the street from Hull House.

Juvenile delinquents:

Young people under the age of 18 who break the law.

A poster advertises a Hull House fund-raiser for Chicago's juvenile court.

Happy Anniversary!

In September 1899, Hull House completed its first decade. What had started as a single house had now grown to a cluster of buildings covering more than a city block. And no one talked about the settlement without linking it to Jane Addams. As early as 1893, she was called the "grandmother of American settlements"—at a time when Jane was only 33 years old.

As the first 10-year chapter in the history of Hull House closed, Jane knew that it was time for her to join a more sweeping reform movement and risk her popularity. She had things to say about free speech, women's rights, and equality for all—subjects guaranteed to cause trouble. She would not be disappointed. Trouble always seems to follow history's change makers.

The original Hull House is surrounded by new buildings.

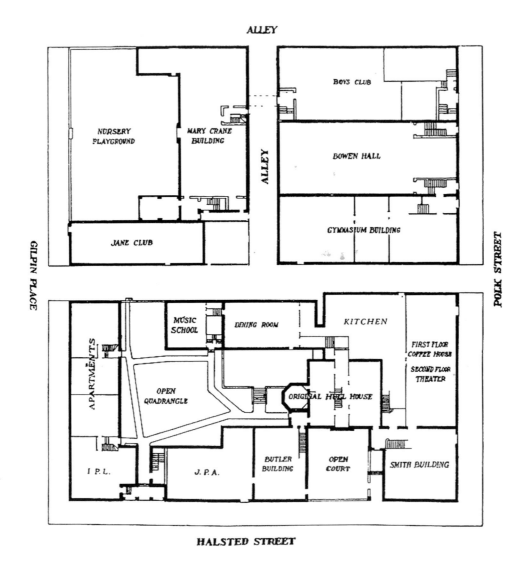

ALLEY

ALLEY

GILPIN PLACE

POLK STREET

NURSERY PLAYGROUND

MARY CRANE BUILDING

JANE CLUB

BOYS CLUB

BOWEN HALL

GYMNASIUM BUILDING

MUSIC SCHOOL

DINING ROOM

KITCHEN

FIRST FLOOR COFFEE HOUSE

SECOND FLOOR THEATER

APARTMENTS

OPEN QUADRANGLE

ORIGINAL HULL HOUSE

I P.L.

J. P. A.

BUTLER BUILDING

OPEN COURT

SMITH BUILDING

HALSTED STREET

Plans of Hull House and two of its later buildings.

Rights

and

Reforms

Chapter 5

1899 - 1912

Key Events in Jane Addams' Life

1900

1901 — Jane protests the arrest of an anarchist newspaper editor following the assassination of President McKinley.

1902

1904

1905

1907 — Jane publishes *Newer Ideals of Peace.*

1908 — Jane protests the killing of a Russian-Jewish immigrant by Chicago's chief of police.

1910 — Jane publishes *Twenty Years at Hull-House.*

1911 — Jane hires a special train to carry more than 300 woman suffrage supporters to Springfield, Illinois.

1912 — Jane and more than 1,000 women travel to Washington, D.C., to pressure Congress on women's voting rights.

1915

1920

Key Events Around the World

1901 — President McKinley dies eight days after being shot by an assassin. Theodore Roosevelt becomes president.

1902 — *McClure's* magazine exposes corruption in U.S. cities and large companies. Its reporters become known as muckrakers.

1904 — The first perfect major-league baseball game is pitched by Cy Young, who does not allow a single player to reach first base.

1905 — Albert Einstein, German physicist, develops his special theory of relativity and the formula $E=mc^2$.

1907 — George W. Goethals and the U.S. Army Corps of Engineers direct construction of the Panama Canal.

1908 — Henry Ford introduces his Model T automobile, which costs $850.

1911 — A fire at the Triangle Shirtwaist Company in New York City kills 146 people, mostly young women.

Jane knew the routine well. Every time a little Italian girl named Angelina showed up for cooking classes at Hull House, she would leave her mother at the front door and run around to a side door. Angelina didn't want to be seen with an immigrant mother who still wore clothes from the homeland—a head kerchief, farming boots, and an Italian skirt.

One evening, Jane broke the young girl's routine. She invited Angelina into the Labor Museum, a center where immigrants worked at crafts such as spinning, weaving, and pottery making. Much to her amazement, Angelina saw a crowd of people surrounding her mother as she used a spindle to spin wool into yarn. Angelina heard people say that her mother was "the best stick-spindle spinner in America."

Jane took the opportunity to tell Angelina about the wonderful skills that immigrants such as her mother brought to America—skills that no machine could match. She asked Angelina to imagine "how hard it must be to . . . give up a beautiful homespun kerchief for an ugly department store hat."

Angelina went home and asked her mother to pull out a trunk of homespun garments she had made in Italy. And from then on, she proudly came into Hull House by the same door as her mother.

Immigrant girls attend a cooking class at Hull House.

Spindle:
A tool used to twist raw wool, cotton, or other natural fibers into thread or yarn.

An Italian woman and her children arrive in the United States in 1900.

A woman demonstrating the spinning of wool at Hull House.

Building Bridges

Jane got the idea for the Labor Museum in 1900. She worried that the gap between immigrants and their Americanized children was growing nearly as wide as the one between immigrants and native-born Americans. The problem gnawed at her as she walked down the street one sunny spring day. Jane had no idea how she might build bridges between these different generations and cultures.

Suddenly, Jane spotted an old woman sitting on the steps of a tenement. Waving a spindle in the air, she told Jane that she soon would have enough yarn to knit a pair of stockings for a young relative.

The old woman gave Jane the clue that she needed. She would build a museum where immigrants could show off skills that could be lost to the machine age. Not only would immigrants gain some recognition for their skills, but their children would learn a new respect for their culture.

Standing Up to Bullies

Hull House tried to teach immigrants to value their place in American democracy. Irish immigrant Francis Hackett summed it up this way:

> *Hull House . . . perceived that the nationalism of each immigrant was a treasure, a talent, which gave him a special value for the United States.*

Not everyone shared that welcoming attitude, however. As millions of immigrants poured into the United States, many people resented the newcomers. Jane believed this prejudice was a great threat to the nation. As she later explained:

One function of the settlement . . . resembled that of a big brother whose mere presence in the playground protected the little ones from bullies.

In 1901, angry Russian Jews asked Jane to intervene with the bullies who had arrested Abraham Isaak, the editor of an anarchist newspaper. He was arrested the same night that a man claiming to be an anarchist shot President William McKinley. Responding to public outrage, the police arrested many innocent people because of their political views. Abraham Isaak's family was rounded up, his printing presses were destroyed, and he was thrown into a dirty jail cell without seeing a lawyer. His outraged neighbors told Jane: "You see what comes of the law you boast of; the authorities will not even let this man see a lawyer!"

The next morning, Jane went directly to the mayor and demanded to see Mr. Isaak. She trudged down a dark stairway to a cell in the jail's basement. Here she found a tired, thin man guarded by 16 policemen. Mr. Isaak again requested a lawyer and asked Jane to find his family.

By now, Hull House was flooded with offers of help. Jane even heard from Clarence Darrow, one of the most famous defense lawyers in America. "I have stood in front of mobs so long that my heart is weary," he wrote, "but I do not see anything else to do and shall not avoid my duty."

Russian immigrants in 1913.

Clarence Darrow.

Chicago police step out of their police wagon with a suspect in 1904.

Eventually, the city released all of the suspects and admitted that they were innocent. But Jane's defense of an anarchist had drawn a firestorm of criticism. As Jane put it: "I . . . discovered that whether or not I had helped a brother out of a pit, I had fallen into a deep one myself."

Although some people praised Jane's courage, many others condemned her. They sent her hate-filled letters and threw rocks through the settlement's windows. But Jane never backed down or changed her position.

"Cousins to the Anarchists"

Several years later, another storm broke loose in Chicago. Early one morning in 1908, a 19-year-old Russian Jew named Averbuch went alone and unarmed to visit the chief of police. As soon as the young man began to speak in halting, broken English, the chief pulled out a gun and shot him four times.

The chief claimed that Averbuch had come to kill him and that he fired in self-defense. His accusation set off another panic. The police arrested Averbuch's sister Olga and hunted for other anarchists. As they searched, they seized or destroyed any foreign-looking items they found, including Jewish religious objects.

Jane got the help of a young lawyer and calmed the anger and fears of the Russian Jews. Trying to turn public opinion against Jane, the chief declared: "Social settlements are first cousins to the anarchists!"

According to Jane's nephew, the police chief's outrageous statement "proved too much for respectable Chicago to stomach." Even though he was never punished for his actions, most people saw him as a coward and a bully.

Battling for Justice

Jane also was sympathetic to the large number of African Americans who had migrated to Chicago from the South. Hull House surveys showed that landlords charged African Americans higher rents than anyone else, forcing them to jam together into small, run-down tenements.

When Jane first started Hull House, the passions and prejudices of the Civil War era still ran high. Jane had been influenced by the views of her father, who was an abolitionist, so she spoke out against postwar injustice and reached out to African Americans in the community around Hull House. The first doctor to live at Hull House was an African American.

As the settlement movement spread, Jane helped to establish the Wendell Philipps Settlement, a project that served African Americans in a nearby racially mixed neighborhood. She also helped to raise money for the Frederick Douglass Center, located in Chicago's South Side. With other Hull House residents, she fought to extend the protection of the juvenile court system to all young people, including African Americans.

At a time when most white Americans ignored racial violence, Jane condemned lynchings in the South. She lashed out at those who claimed that "these . . . terrorizing acts have been committed . . . to make the lives and honor of [white] women safe." Speaking as a woman, Jane exclaimed:

Chicago children stand outside one of the small apartments that were available to African Americans.

Abolitionist:

Someone dedicated to ending slavery. Some abolitionists also established programs that provided education and employment for African Americans.

Lynchings:

Unlawful executions by hanging without a trial by jury, usually racially motivated.

Booker T. Washington.

Top: Ida Wells-Barnett.

NAACP:

An organization founded in 1909 to protect the rights and welfare of all people of color.

Civil-rights movement:

An organized social movement to win equal rights for African Americans and other minority groups.

"The honor of women is only secure . . . where law and order and justice prevail!"

Such hard-hitting speeches earned Jane the respect of a number of African-American leaders, including Ida Wells-Barnett and Booker T. Washington. In 1909, Jane became one of several whites to sit on the executive board of the newly founded National Association for the Advancement of Colored People (NAACP). Jane supported the work of NAACP lawyers who battled injustices in the courts and who became the first leaders of a new civil-rights movement.

"I Have No Vote"

In 1909, the same year that Jane joined the NAACP, President Theodore Roosevelt invited her to speak at a White House conference. As the time neared for the speakers to appear onstage, a flustered young aide blurted out: "Are we all here? Yes, here is my Catholic speaker, my Jewish speaker, the Protestant, the colored man, and the woman. Let's all go on."

Jane turned to her good friend Booker T. Washington ("the colored man") and said: "You see, I am last; that is because I have no vote."

He replied: "I am glad to know the reason. I have always . . . been [at] the end of such a procession myself."

Although President Roosevelt found the incident amusing, it is doubtful that Jane felt the same way. Living in the slums had convinced her that women needed the vote to protect themselves and their children from social evils such as poverty, filthy streets, and unsafe working conditions.

Jane was late in joining the woman suffrage movement. Hull House projects had taken so much of her time that she did not attend a meeting of the National American Woman Suffrage Association (NAWSA) until 1906. At this meeting, Jane delivered a powerful speech on why women should vote. She also met Susan B. Anthony, one of the movement's founders.

In 1911, Jane became vice president of NAWSA. That year she helped to launch a major campaign for woman suffrage in Illinois. Along with her Rockford classmate Catharine Waugh McCulloch, Jane hired a special train to carry more than 300 suffragettes from Chicago to the state capital in Springfield. The suffragettes made speeches at every stop along the way. When they arrived in Springfield, they pressured Illinois legislators to vote on a suffrage bill. Despite their efforts, the bill was defeated.

The following year, Jane led a delegation of more than 1,000 women to Washington, D.C., to pressure Congress to give women the vote. Jane handpicked the speakers who would testify, but in the end, Congress denied the NAWSA request for a suffrage amendment to the Constitution.

Jane did not give up the fight. She even appeared in a vaudeville show and in a silent movie to spread the word about woman suffrage. These public appearances made Jane a natural choice to represent NAWSA at the 1912 Republican presidential convention. She hoped to persuade the party of Abraham Lincoln and her father to adopt a platform supporting woman suffrage.

Jane Addams speaks about woman suffrage from the back of a train in Illinois in 1911.

Suffrage:
The right to vote.

Suffragettes:
Women who campaigned for the right to vote.

Amendment:
An addition to the U.S. Constitution that changes or clarifies its original meaning. It must be approved by a two-thirds majority vote in Congress and by two-thirds of the state governments.

Vaudeville:
A live stage show, popular in the early 1900s, usually consisting of slapstick comedy, music, and dance.

Theodore Roosevelt.

Conservatives:

People who believe that the role of the government is less important than individual or states' rights.

Progressive movement:

A reform movement in the early 1900s that supported a return of government control to the people, expanded economic opportunities, and improved social conditions.

Pacifist:

A person who is opposed to war or violence of any kind.

A New Political Party

The Republican convention promised an all-out political battle for the party's presidential nomination. Theodore Roosevelt (nicknamed TR) had stepped down from the presidency in 1909. He turned the office over to his handpicked successor, William Howard Taft. By 1912, TR wanted his job back. He felt that President Taft had neglected his reform programs. Not all Republicans agreed, and a huge split developed among party members.

Jane and NAWSA added fuel to the fire with their demands for suffrage. The Republican platform committee gave Jane seven minutes to present her case but took no action. The convention belonged to Republican conservatives, who rejected TR and woman suffrage. TR and his supporters stormed out of the convention, vowing to form a new political party.

True to his word, TR formed the Progressive Party. He hoped the name would appeal to reform-minded Americans—Republicans and Democrats alike—who made up the Progressive movement. TR wanted Jane Addams and other well-known reformers by his side. He had to work hard to win Jane's support, however, because the two of them disagreed strongly over issues of war and peace.

Rough Rider vs. Pacifist

Jane opposed all war. Her strong beliefs went back to the 1890s when she had read the writings of Russian pacifist Leo Tolstoy. Jane had been inspired to visit Russia in 1896 and talk with the author in person. Tolstoy had challenged Jane to explain how a wealthy woman like herself could ever hope to understand the poor. He then planted a disturbing thought in her mind. He warned that without international peace there could never be human progress—not even at Hull House.

When the Spanish-American War broke out in 1898, Tolstoy's words came back to haunt Jane. She had watched with horror as children played war in the streets. Instead of celebrating the U.S. victory in the war, Jane had grieved that there had been a war in the first place.

Her feelings had put her at odds with TR. He had ridden to fame as a Rough Rider in the Spanish-American War. When he campaigned for president in 1903, Jane said: "There are many things that I admire about President Roosevelt, but I object to voting for him or for any man on a 'war record.'"

TR had the same mixed feelings about Jane. He admired her achievements as a reformer, but he objected to her antiwar sentiments.

From 1903 to 1907, Jane wrote a book about her beliefs called *Newer Ideals of Peace*. While she worked on her book, TR was busy taking control of the Panama Canal, warning European powers to stay out of the Americas, and sending a fleet of U.S. battleships around the world. It may have seemed ironic to Jane that he won the Nobel Peace Prize in 1906 for helping to end a war between Japan and Russia.

When TR read Jane's antiwar book in 1907, he exploded in anger. He called her "foolish Jane Addams" and charged that she lacked the "strength, training, and natural ability" to understand "the teachings of a man like Tolstoy."

Meeting Leo Tolstoy

When Jane Addams visited the Russian writer Leo Tolstoy in 1896, she wore the dress in the photo above. But Tolstoy's reaction shocked Jane. Looking at the sleeves of her dress, he said, "There is enough stuff on one arm to make a frock for a little girl. Do you not find such a dress a barrier to the people?"

Jane Addams (right) riding in a woman suffrage parade, around 1910.

In the end, TR and Jane made peace with each other. Jane knew that TR had the political power to fight for the social reforms that she supported. TR knew that Jane could rally the votes of people who admired her, especially immigrants, African Americans, and members of labor unions.

In June 1912, TR approached Jane with an offer. If she would join the Progressive Party, he would support woman suffrage. Jane soon found herself on the party's platform committee, hammering out her ideas for the future.

PRESIDENT
HOW LONG
MUST
WOMEN WAIT
FOR LIBERTY

U of MO.

WASHINGTON COLLEGE

LELAND STANFORD

BRYN MAWR

SWARTHMORE

VASSAR

MR.PRESIDENT
WHAT
WILL YOU
FOR
WOMAN SUFFRAGE

PEACE

Speaking Out

Chapter 6

1912 - 1915

Key Events in Jane Addams' Life

Key Events Around the World

1910

1912

Jane attends the Progressive Party convention in Chicago. She travels across America speaking about her favorite causes.

The passenger ship *Titanic* strikes an iceberg in the Atlantic Ocean and sinks, killing more than 1,500 people, many of them immigrants traveling to America.

1913

Jane travels to Europe to attend an international woman suffrage convention.

1914

Ford Motor Company sets up the first assembly line and is able to produce 1,000 Model T cars a day.

1915

Jane begins her crusade to keep America from joining the war in Europe.

British explorer Ernest Shackleton leads an expedition to Antarctica.

Jane attends an international women's peace congress in The Hague, capital of the Netherlands.

The British ship *Lusitania* is sunk by a German submarine in the Atlantic. Some 1,200 passengers die.

1920

1925

1930

Baroness Bertha von Suttner blasted Jane Addams for supporting Theodore Roosevelt. An Austrian pacifist, she was the first woman to win the Nobel Peace Prize. In an open letter to the world, she accused Jane of joining an antipeace organization that favored "the ancient and barbaric system of justice called war."

But Jane saw peace as more than the absence of war. Jane claimed that in 1912 more people were dying in the factories than on the battlefields. She then rattled off numbers to support her position: 15,000 workers killed in factories every year and another half million crippled.

In Jane's opinion, TR's Progressive Party was "on the road to world peace" through its pledge to prevent "industrial accidents, occupational diseases, overwork, . . . unemployment, and other . . . effects of modern industry." Even if the party lost the election, Jane felt she could use the campaign to promote social justice.

Jane Addams in 1913 at age 53.

Bitter Trade-Offs

When the Progressive Party held its convention in Chicago in 1912, Jane persuaded TR to support a number of issues. These included an eight-hour workday, a six-day workweek, improved housing conditions, a ban on child labor under age 16, and the protection of women workers. He also accepted word for word a suffrage statement written by Jane:

A young boy works at a large factory machine in 1908.

A 1912 political cartoon showing the three-way race to the White House. TR's Progressive Party was also known as the Bull Moose Party.

The Progressive Party, believing that no people can justly claim to be a true democracy which denies political rights on the account of sex, pledges itself to the task of securing equal suffrage to men and women alike.

But the former Rough Rider refused to give up his battleships. After a brief flurry of opposition, the platform committee approved plans for two of them. Jane later admitted: "I found it very difficult to swallow those two battleships."

Jane found it even more difficult to accept another TR decision. He wanted to allow several southern states to have only white delegates. Jane thought that every state should have some African-American delegates. She also believed the party platform should support African-American rights.

TR argued that he would lose the South—and the election—if he forced either issue. Jane, the daughter of an abolitionist, struggled with her conscience. She and Henry Moskowitz, a New York settlement worker, were the only ones to speak out against TR's position. Jane declared:

Some of us are very much disturbed that this Progressive party which stands for human rights, should . . . appear not to stand for the rights of [African Americans].

Jane almost left the party over the matter of African-American rights. She stayed only because she refused to abandon woman suffrage and labor reform. When TR asked her to second his nomination at the convention, Jane agreed. She welcomed a chance to present her ideas on social justice to the entire nation.

"Our Prize Exhibit"

On August 7, 1912, thousands of reformers packed the Chicago Coliseum to witness the moment when TR accepted the nomination of his new political party. Progressive journalist William Allen White noted the number of women present:

> [W]omen doctors, women lawyers, women teachers, college professors, middle-aged leaders of civic movements, or rich young girls who had gone in for settlement work.

He then added: "Our prize exhibit was Jane Addams."

New York City party boss William Prendergast placed TR's name before the convention. Delegates went wild. When Jane Addams stood to second the nomination, the Coliseum erupted in a foot-stomping, hand-clapping tribute to the nation's best-known reformer.

Dressed in white, Jane spoke quietly and calmly. She devoted most of her time to praising the party's platform. "A great party," said Jane, "has pledged itself to the protection of children, to the care of the aged, to the relief of overworked girls, to the safeguarding of burdened men."

Women march for voting rights in a 1912 suffrage parade.

She waited until the very end of her speech to mention the candidate. In carefully chosen words, Jane endorsed TR for his broad support of reform.

When Jane stepped down from the speaker's platform, the crowd shouted and cheered—more for Jane herself than for TR. A group of women jumped to their feet and unfolded a yellow banner that read "VOTES FOR WOMEN." They marched behind Jane in a spontaneous parade. Although others spoke at the convention, Jane's speech received the most attention. "This speech," proclaimed the *Congressional Record,* "was the entrance of women into national politics."

Next Jane hit the campaign trail. She traveled more than 7,500 miles, speaking for her favorite causes. When a reporter asked if the platform alone interested her, Jane replied: "It is the platform we women care about." Then, with a smile, she added: "We are so glad to have so distinguished a man [as TR] to lead our cause."

In the end, the election went to the Democratic candidate, New Jersey governor Woodrow Wilson. The outcome did not surprise Jane. As she told a reporter: "I had expected from the beginning that Mr. Wilson was to be the next President of the United States." What mattered to her was having the opportunity to capture national attention for reform issues. Jane believed that the new president, who considered himself a progressive, would soon take up these same issues himself.

President Woodrow Wilson.

Exhausted by the campaign, Jane planned to travel in Europe and Egypt with her friend Mary Rozet Smith. While in Europe, she wanted to attend the meeting of the International Woman Suffrage Association in Budapest, Hungary. She boarded a ship in Vienna, Austria, for a leisurely cruise down the Danube River to Hungary. In June 1913, Jane had no idea that she was traveling through an area that would soon become a war zone. As she later wrote:

> Not a breath, not a tremor of the future, ruffled the polished surface of the Danube on that summer's day. There was no [fear] that these bordering states within a year's time would be firing the opening shots of the most terrible war recorded in history.

The War against War

World War I arrived on Jane's doorstep suddenly and dramatically. In August 1914, just two days after Jane learned of the war, a huge German tanker appeared in the waters near her summer cottage in Bar Harbor, Maine. The captain had dropped anchor to escape warships in the Atlantic. The sight of this huge, out-of-place ship, said Jane, "was the first fantastic impression of . . . a changed world."

The "changed world" of 1914 frightened Jane. Competing for empires and trade, the nations of Europe had formed rival alliances, ready for battle at a moment's notice. That moment came on June 28, 1914, when a Serbian nationalist shot Archduke Francis Ferdinand—the

Alliances:
Groups of nations that promise to join together to fight a common enemy.

Nationalist:
A person who puts the interests of his or her own country first.

Archduke Francis Ferdinand and his wife.

heir to the throne of Austria-Hungary—and his wife, Sophie. The assassination set off an international explosion. In a matter of weeks, all of the major European nations were pulled into war. On one side were the Central Powers, led by Germany, Austria-Hungry, and Turkey. On the other side were the Allies, led by Britain, France, and Russia.

Never before had nations used the full power of the Industrial Revolution to kill one another. Machine guns, poison gas, tanks, and heavy artillery turned the war front into a deadly no man's land. Jane agreed that even child labor seemed a "little thing" when compared with the "wholesale slaughter of thousands of men a day."

Jane vowed to use her influence to oppose war as a means of settling human differences. If it was human nature to fight, said Jane, then people should be taught to fight social evils such as hunger, poverty, and disease—not one another.

When Jane decided to declare war on war, she was one of the most admired people in the nation. She was well known from her lectures and speeches, and from her column in *The Ladies' Home Journal* and the books she had published. She was more popular than many men of her time, even presidents. But in 1914, she placed her reputation on the line by asking Americans to join her on the path of peace.

No man's land

A barren strip of land between opposing lines of soldiers on a battlefield.

Jane Addams, around 1914.

Crusade for Peace

In late September 1914, Jane started her crusade for peace at the Henry Street Settlement in New York City. Most of the members of the so-called Henry Street group had lived or worked at a settlement. Jane believed that social workers, more than any other group in America, could imagine world peace. As she later explained:

> All of us, through long experiences among the immigrants from many nations, were convinced that a friendly and cooperative relationship was constantly becoming more possible between all peoples.

The group wanted to go beyond President Wilson's policy of neutrality by taking a stronger stand against war. One member even expressed a willingness to go to jail rather than pick up a gun. Together they explored ways to end the war and to influence a peace settlement. To oppose military buildups by the United States, they formed the American Union Against Militarism.

A short time after the meeting, women's rights leader Carrie Chapman Catt asked Jane to help organize a women's peace conference in Washington, D.C. The plan was inspired by Rosika Schwimmer, a Hungarian firebrand who promoted international peace and woman suffrage. Jane had some doubts about an all-women's peace organization, but the outpouring of support was so strong that Jane could not refuse.

Social workers:
People trained to improve the social conditions within a community.

Neutrality:
The policy of not taking sides in disagreements between other nations, especially during times of war.

Firebrand:
A nickname for people who boldly speak out about particular causes and issues.

Carrie Chapman Catt.

Preamble:

The introductory part of a speech, document, or story.

Cablegram:

An overseas telegram transmitted through a cable underwater.

The Hague:

The capital of the Netherlands; also, a center for the promotion of peace located there.

Jane (second from left, in front), with other members of her peace delegation sailing to the Netherlands.

On January 10, 1915, about 3,000 women gathered in the ballroom of the new Willard Hotel in Washington. Nearly everyone looked to Jane for leadership. She delivered the opening speech, served as chair, and helped to draft the group's peace platform. The preamble, written by Anna Garland Spencer, declared:

> We, [the] women of the United States, assembled in behalf of World Peace, grateful for the security of our own country, but sorrowing for the misery of all involved in the present struggle among warring nations, do hereby band ourselves together to demand that war be abolished. . . .

The platform called for an immediate meeting of neutral nations to create a peace plan, a limit on weapons, universal woman suffrage, a world organization to settle international disputes, and a police force to enforce global law. The women planned to present their platform first to President Wilson, then to the world. As it turned out, the world came to them first.

"Willing to Fail"

In February 1915, Jane received a cablegram from Alleta Jacobs, a suffrage leader who was one of the first women doctors in Holland. Dr. Jacobs invited her to attend an international women's peace congress at The Hague in the Netherlands. The goal of the congress was to involve women from neutral and warring nations in a plan for peace.

Jane admired the organizers of the congress, calling them "women of great courage and ability." She hoped the congress of women would be able to hammer out a framework for peace. But she also worried that it might be a "flat failure." In the end, Jane bet on the cause of peace. "Women who are willing to fail," she explained, "may be able to break through that . . . spell which makes it impossible for any of the nations to consider peace."

Jane quickly rounded up a delegation of 42 women. On April 12, they set sail for the Netherlands. The trip was dangerous because German submarines prowled the ocean. Just off the coast of England, a British gunboat aimed a machine gun at the ship, insisting that it be searched before heading into Allied waters. "Just think of Jane Addams with a machine gun trained on her," remarked one of the passengers.

To relieve the tension of the journey, the women turned the ship into a floating classroom. They held lectures and classes on the peace movement three times a day. They huddled on the proposals that they would put before the convention. Jane described the experience of working with like-minded women as a "precious moment."

When they arrived at The Hague, the women joined delegates from 12 nations: Austria, Belgium, Canada, Denmark, Germany, Great Britain, Hungary, Italy, the Netherlands, Norway, Sweden, and the United States. Delegates spoke several different languages and introduced many resolutions. However, they stood united in their desire to end the war. The delegates looked to Jane for leadership. As chair, she brought order to the proceedings. Time and again, she inspired women with her speeches, which she gave in French, German, or Italian.

Jane (second from left, in front), among members of the First International Congress of Women, The Hague, in 1915.

The only person who could outdo Jane's eloquence was Rosika Schwimmer, who could speak even more languages than Jane. Near the end of the meeting, Rosika swept the women off their feet with a plan to take their peace proposals directly to world leaders. The proposals stressed the need for neutral nations to negotiate peace, the formation of an international congress of nations after the war, and worldwide voting rights for women.

Jane wondered if the plan could succeed. "There is just one chance in 10 thousand," she wrote. However, when she saw how important it was to the women of Europe, she reluctantly agreed to be one of the messengers.

Carrying the Message

The women's peace congress selected two groups to "carry the message." One group, led by Jane Addams and Alleta Jacobs, set out to visit the capitals of warring nations. The other group, led by Rosika Schwimmer, made its way to the capitals of neutral nations.

Just two days before Jane left The Hague, tragedy struck. At 2:10 p.m. on May 7, 1915, a German U-boat fired a single torpedo at the British ship *Lusitania*. Nearly 1,200 people died, including more than 100 Americans.

U-boat:
Short for Unterseeboot, the German word for submarine.

Jane's doubts about the peace mission were doubled by the *Lusitania* sinking. Even so, she went ahead with the mission and came face to face with each nation's determination to win the war. She also got a firsthand look at bombed-out buildings, wounded soldiers, and starving civilians.

Jane's group met with eight prime ministers or presidents, nine foreign ministers, and the Pope. With the exception of France, the nation hardest hit by German invasions, Jane was surprised to find that most nations were willing to listen. She later reported, "Each one said that his country would be ready to stop the war immediately if some honorable method of securing peace were provided."

The most enthusiastic response came from Prime Minister Karl von Stürgkh of Austria. When Jane finished her presentation, he remained silent. Fumbling for words, Jane continued: "It perhaps seems to you very foolish that women should go about in this way."

At this, the minister banged his fist on a table and cried: "Foolish? Not at all. These are the first sensible words that have been uttered in this room for ten months."

But such triumphs were fleeting. Jane realized that none of the warring nations would start peace talks on their own. As she sadly admitted, "They were all of the opinion that this war was inevitable." The only hope of peace was for a neutral nation to call a peace conference. Jane believed that nation should be the United States. So on June 24, after weeks of travel, Jane set sail for home.

An illustration showing the sinking of the *Lusitania*, in 1915.

The U.S. passport Jane took to the peace conference in The Hague, in 1915.

Base:
Lacking dignity or morality.

"Welcome Home Jane Addams"

Jane's ship docked in New York harbor on July 5. She was greeted by about 50 people wearing white ribbons that said "Welcome Home Jane Addams." Not all Americans were quite so glad to see her return, however. Sympathy for the Allies had been growing steadily, and the sinking of the *Lusitania* had enflamed passions for war. Although most people praised Jane for her idealism, others were hostile—and Theodore Roosevelt was the most hostile of all.

The former president was itching to get into the war. In a letter to one of the women who traveled to The Hague, he wrote: "Pacifists are cowards, and your scheme is both silly and base." TR did not single out Jane in his attack—at least not yet. Too many people still admired her.

That admiration would soon change. So many people would turn against Jane that TR would call her "poor bleeding Jane" and "one of the shrieking sisterhood." Other people would call her even worse names—like traitor!

Standing Alone

Chapter 7

1915- 1918

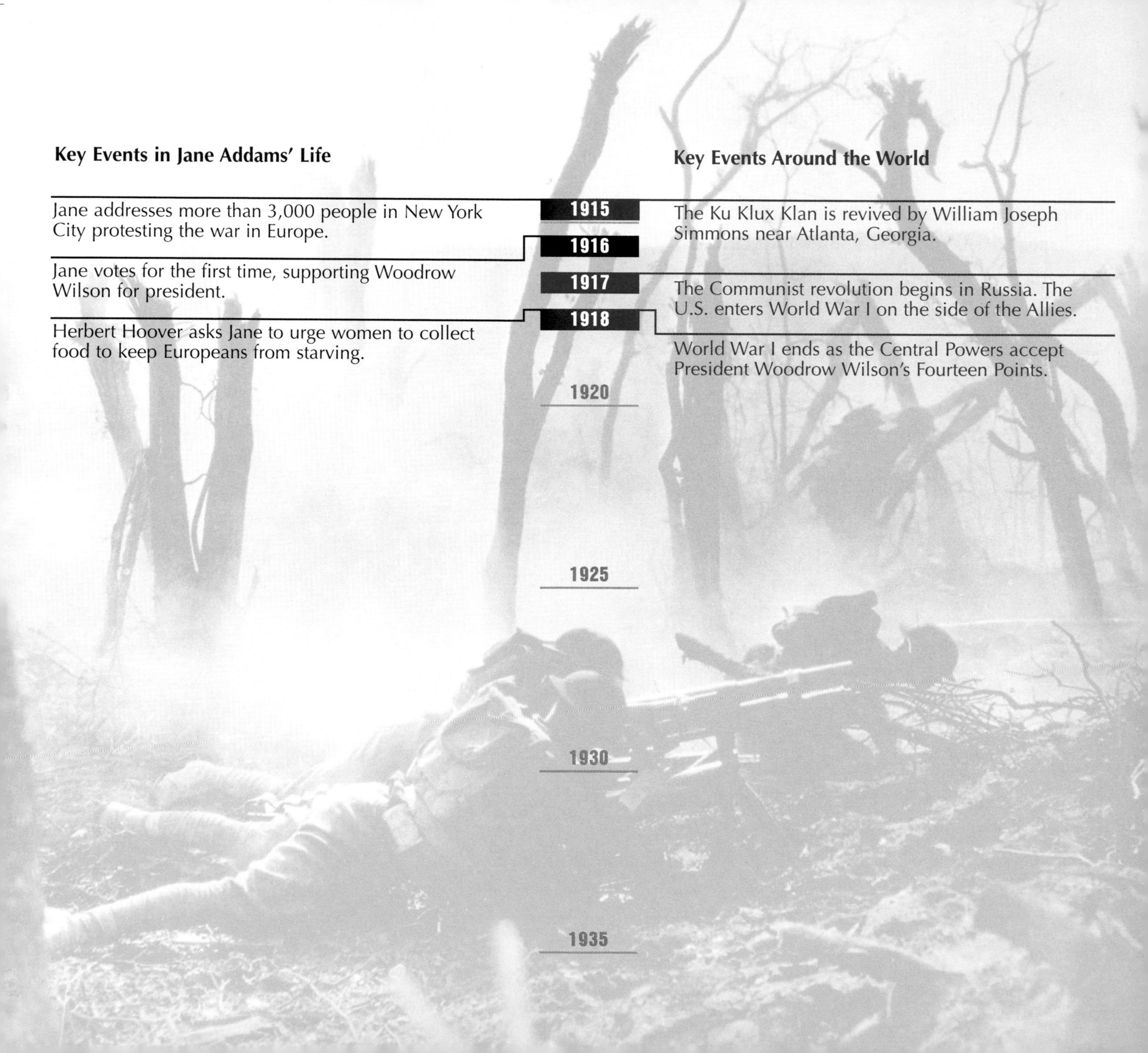

Key Events in Jane Addams' Life

Jane addresses more than 3,000 people in New York City protesting the war in Europe.

Jane votes for the first time, supporting Woodrow Wilson for president.

Herbert Hoover asks Jane to urge women to collect food to keep Europeans from starving.

Key Events Around the World

1915

The Ku Klux Klan is revived by William Joseph Simmons near Atlanta, Georgia.

1916

1917

The Communist revolution begins in Russia. The U.S. enters World War I on the side of the Allies.

1918

World War I ends as the Central Powers accept President Woodrow Wilson's Fourteen Points.

1920

1925

1930

1935

Jane Addams, around 1915.

*S*ome Americans still wanted to hear what Jane Addams had to say about the war in Europe. On July 9, 1915, she spoke at New York City's Carnegie Hall. Theodore Roosevelt was invited, but he refused to attend.

As Jane stared out at the large crowd, she arranged a few notes in front of her. She had decided to speak from her heart and mind—not from a prepared speech. Jane explained that it was difficult to imagine peace "when brought face to face with so much genuine emotion and high patriotism as Europe exhibits at the present moment." Unless a neutral power intervened, said Jane, the war would be long and bitter.

Jane also felt the need to tell the story of the war from the soldier's point of view. In a calm, steady voice, she declared:

Generally speaking, we heard everywhere that this war was an old man's war; that the young men who were dying, the young men who were fighting, were not the men who wanted the war, and were not the men who believed in the war.

Jane gave specific examples. She told of a young Swiss soldier who refused to fire his gun "in a way that could possibly hit another man." She spoke of five wounded German soldiers who committed suicide rather than go back to the front. "[T]hey were not afraid of being killed," explained Jane, "they were afraid they might be put in a position where they would have to kill someone else."

Jane's words shocked the audience. Warring leaders, she continued, had discovered the need to issue a "stimulant before the men would engage in bayonet charges . . . they have a regular formula in Germany . . . they give them rum in England and absinthe in France."

Absinthe:
A strong, bitter alcoholic drink banned by many countries in the 1900s.

Jane could not have been more misunderstood. The next day, newspaper headlines like this one exploded all over the country:

TROOPS DRINK-CRAZED, SAYS MISS ADDAMS

The main point of her talk—that warring nations would be grateful if neutral countries intervened—was entirely lost. Also lost was Jane's reputation.

A Damaged Reputation

After her Carnegie Hall speech, criticism rained down on Jane from all directions. She had attacked the image of the brave soldier who shouldered a gun and headed courageously into battle. Instead, Jane had described the gut-wrenching fear of soldiers running at one another with steel bayonets. She had argued that some soldiers loathed killing so much that they could never bring themselves to fire at an enemy.

War correspondent Richard Harding Davis led the battle against Jane. In a letter to the *New York Times,* he defended the Allied soldier:

> *Miss Addams denies him the credit of his sacrifice. She strips him of honor and courage. She tells his children, "Your father did not die for France, or for England, or for you; he died because he was drunk."*

Other newspapers jumped into the battle. They used such terms as "pitiful failure" and "silly, vain, old maid." Yet another concluded:

A makeshift hospital in a bombed-out church during World War I.

If Jane Addams is a careful reader of the newspapers, she must have discovered by this time that a popular idol can be knocked from [her] pedestal by talking too much.

A few newspapers sided with Jane, and some fellow pacifists sent her letters of support. But most of the mail that poured into Hull House criticized her. Although saddened by the outburst, Jane refused to attack her attackers. As she explained years later:

[I]t was at this time that I first learned to use . . . a statement of Booker T. Washington's. "I will permit no man to make me to hate him."

Jane Addams at about age 55.

Voting for Peace

During the summer and fall of 1915, Jane continued to campaign for a peace conference of neutral nations. She repeatedly tried to meet with President Wilson. When she finally got an appointment, the president politely accepted a copy of resolutions from the Women's Peace Party, but he took no action.

By this time Jane was 55 years old and in declining health. She suffered from bouts of pneumonia and an infection that led to the removal of one of her kidneys.

Despite her health problems, she again traveled to Washington, D.C., in January 1916, to testify against a military buildup called for by Congress. She also visited President Wilson once more. As they talked, the president pulled out a well-worn copy of the resolutions Jane had

Jane (center), Julia Lathrop (left), and Mary McDowell (right) travel to Washington, D.C., to meet with the president.

19th Amendment:
The amendment to the U.S. Constitution giving women the right to vote; it was passed by Congress in 1919 and added to the Constitution in 1920.

Mandate:
An overwhelming vote in favor of a particular action.

given him earlier. "You see I have studied these resolutions," he said. "I consider them by far the best formulation which up to the moment has been put out by anybody."

Peace was the central issue of the 1916 presidential campaign. Although public opinion favored the Allies, most Americans still wanted to stay out of the war. President Wilson campaigned on the slogan He Kept Us Out of War. His supporters tried to paint his Republican opponent, Charles Evans Hughes, as a war candidate. Both men wanted the voters to think that they stood for peace, so both tried to win Jane's support.

They wanted Jane's support for another reason. In 1916, Jane finally could vote! Three years earlier, Illinois had passed a woman suffrage law—seven years before the 19th Amendment to the Constitution was ratified.

Jane struggled with her conscience. She did not always agree with President Wilson's decisions. But Wilson had promoted some progressive legislation, including child labor laws, and he really had kept the nation out of the war in Europe.

In the end, Jane cast her vote for President Wilson. He sent her a warm letter of thanks and invited her to dinner at the White House. She later recalled:

> *It seemed at last, as if peace were assured and the future safe in the hands of a chief executive who had received a mandate from the people "to keep us out of war."*

War!

Jane's hopes soared again in December 1916 when President Wilson asked warring nations to name their terms for peace. In January 1917, he delivered his famous Peace without Victory speech, calling for an end to the war before either side achieved victory. He also proposed an international peacekeeping organization. Jane sent Wilson a telegram congratulating him on his "brilliant statement."

But President Wilson had waited too long to take a stand. On January 31, 1917, Germany announced that it would begin unrestricted submarine warfare in the Atlantic. This meant that its U-boats might sink American ships. Four days later, President Wilson broke off all diplomatic relations with the Germans.

Jane made a last, desperate attempt to avoid war. She formed the Emergency Peace Federation, which sponsored letter-writing campaigns and parades at the White House. She also had one final meeting with the president. This time, Wilson turned his back on her entirely. In a speech delivered on March 12, 1917, the president declared:

> *What I am opposed to is not the feeling of the pacifists. . . . My heart is with them. I want peace, but I know how to get it and they do not.*

After three U.S. ships had been sunk by the Germans, President Wilson told Americans, "The world must be made safe for democracy." On April 2, 1917, he asked Congress for a formal declaration of war. Jane now faced an agonizing decision. Would she remain a pacifist? Or would she support the war?

A political cartoon showing President Wilson's changed policy on the war in Europe.

Robert Carter illustration courtesy of CORBIS/Bettmann, BE031442.

A parade of people supporting America's entry into World War I, in Aurora, Missouri, April 1917.

Taking a Stand

For more than two months, Jane kept her silence. Then, on June 10 she delivered a public speech, "Pacifism and Patriotism in Time of War." Jane insisted that pacifists were not cowards or traitors. She also spoke kindly of German immigrants in the United States. Finally, she defended the need for an international peacekeeping organization to avoid future wars.

When she finished, no one applauded. Judge Orrin Carter, a strong supporter of Hull House, rose to speak. "I have been a lifelong friend of Miss Addams," he declared. "I have agreed with her on most questions, in the past, but—"

"That 'but' sounds ominous," said Jane with a faint smile. "It sounds like you're going to break with me."

With emotion, Judge Carter said he *was* going to break with her. Then he added, "I think anything that may tend to cast doubt on the justice of our cause in the present war is very unfortunate."

On that sour note, the meeting abruptly ended. The next day, newspapers around the country denounced Jane as a traitor. One by one, many of her friends, including people at Hull House, lined up behind the war effort. Jane felt very alone. Years later, she confessed that the nationwide criticism "brought me very near to self pity, perhaps the lowest pit into which human nature can sink."

A Matter of Conscience

Jane found little comfort at Hull House. Swept up by wartime patriotism, many of its men enlisted to fight. When Congress passed a draft law, Jane reluctantly allowed a draft board at the settlement. She regretted her decision when one of the young immigrants said it was Jane's fault that he had been drafted to fight. "I really have you to thank if I am sent over to Europe to fight," he said. "I went into the citizenship class in the first place because you asked me to. If I hadn't . . . I would be exempt."

Jane struggled to find words of comfort. But the young man was right. Jane had talked many immigrants into becoming citizens. In sorrow, she declared:

> All that had been told them of the American freedom, which
> they had hoped to secure for themselves and their children, had
> turned to ashes.

Jane longed to relieve the suffering of war, but she had lost her audience. Few Americans wanted to join in any program that she supported. In late 1917, Jane discovered that she was being watched by the Department of Justice. In a moment of doubt, she asked: "Has the individual . . . the right to stand out against millions of his fellow countrymen?" In matters of conscience, Jane knew the answer was yes.

As thousands of U.S. soldiers headed overseas, Jane searched for a way to help them without supporting the war. Herbert Hoover offered a solution. Hoover was the head of the Department of Food Administration, which had been organized in 1917 to distribute food to war-torn Belgium. He had grown up in the Quaker tradition, as had Jane.

Draft law:

A law requiring service in the military for all eligible males; it is usually activated during times of war.

Exempt:

Not eligible.

Immigrants studying to be American citizens at a class in Hull House.

Wallace Kirkland photo courtesy of Univesity of Illinois at Chicago, neg. 261.

American soldiers capture the village of Exermont, in France, in November 1918, a few days before the end of World War I.

In early 1918, he asked Jane to urge women to collect food and grow more crops to keep Europeans from starving.

Jane jumped at the chance to do something useful. She toured the nation, speaking at high schools, women's clubs, and public meetings. Americans seemed ready to forgive her for what one newspaper described as her "mistaken activities" in the name of peace. "Now she is seeing clearly again," the *Los Angeles Times* declared, "and her service is with the country, with the administration, with the Allies."

But Jane had not budged one bit on the peace issue. In a letter to her niece she stated: "[M]y convictions are not changing, nor wavering." When World War I finally ended in November 1918, Jane Addams began speaking again for the cause of peace and freedom.

Still
Pioneering

Chapter 8   1918 - 1935

Key Events in Jane Addams' Life

Key Events Around the World

1915

1919

Jane travels to Zurich, Switzerland, for the second international women's peace congress.

Congress adopts the 19th Amendment to the U.S. Constitution, granting American women the right to vote.

1920

Jane joins other social reformers to form the American Civil Liberties Union to protect First Amendment freedoms.

1921

U.S. suffragist Carrie Chapman Catt creates the League of Women Voters to provide women with information about candidates.

1922

A Paris conference of Allies forces Germany to pay a heavy price of $33 billion for war damages.

1924

Philo T. Farnsworth, a 15-year-old Utah schoolboy, designs a system that is later developed into television.

1925

Congress grants full U.S. citizenship rights to Native Americans, including the right to vote.

1928

Jane chairs a meeting of the Pan-Pacific Women's Union in Honolulu, Hawaii.

Scottish scientist Alexander Fleming discovers penicillin, a medicine that will help fight some of the world's worst diseases.

1930

Jane publishes *The Second Twenty Years at Hull-House.*
Jane holds a three-day reunion for some of the people helped by Hull House.

1931

The Star-Spangled Banner, written in 1814 by Francis Scott Key, becomes the U.S. national anthem.

1932

Jane and U.S. educator Nicholas M. Butler share the Nobel Peace Prize.

Presidential candidate Franklin D. Roosevelt calls for a New Deal for all Americans.

1935

Jane Addams dies in Chicago, Illinois, at age 74.

President Roosevelt signs the Social Security Act, establishing old-age insurance funded by a tax on both workers and employers.

As soon as the fighting stopped, Jane helped to plan the second international women's peace congress. The meeting was scheduled for May 12, 1919, in the neutral city of Zurich, Switzerland.

On her way, Jane planned to stop in northern France. She hoped to find the grave of her nephew John Linn, a chaplain killed by an artillery shell while carrying food to soldiers in foxholes.

In early April, Jane and her friend Dr. Alice Hamilton arrived in Paris and set out to visit the battlefield where her nephew had fallen. Everywhere they traveled, they saw the effects of war—mounds of artillery shells, broken-down tanks, rusted coils of barbed wire, and deep, muddy trenches.

Near Argonne, the place where John had died, Jane and Alice searched through the huge temporary graveyards. When Jane finally located the grave, she said a tearful good-bye. She remembered the words from one of her nephew's last letters. "I will probably be killed," he wrote, "but if I am not I shall not come back. There will be too much to do over here that is worthwhile."

Jane and Alice tried to imagine what young men like John had endured on the battlefields. No, they had not been wrong in opposing war, and they were not wrong in returning to Europe. Like her nephew, Jane believed that there was much worthwhile work to be done. She headed for Zurich to find out what that work should be.

Dr. Alice Hamilton, Hull House resident and specialist in industrial diseases.

Foxholes:
Holes dug in a battlefield to provide cover for soldiers.

American soldiers marching through the Argonne region of France in 1919, soon after the end of World War I.

The Women's International League for Peace and Freedom, in Zurich, Switzerland, in 1919. Jane is third from the right in the front row.

Blockade:

A line of military equipment or soldiers that prevents any communication or trade from within or outside an enemy port or border.

Treaty of Versailles:

The peace agreement in 1919 that ended World War I; it demanded huge war payments from Germany.

Healing the World

On her first day in Zurich, Jane saw an Austrian woman who had been a delegate to the earlier conference at The Hague in 1915. "She was so shrunken and changed that I had much difficulty in identifying her as the beautiful woman I had seen three years before," declared Jane.

That night, the Austrian woman told Jane what it was like to live on the edge of starvation. A person thought about nothing but food, she said. As the woman spoke, Jane remembered the starving children that she had seen in northern France. The hungry people of Europe had to be fed, she concluded.

Jane found a ready audience for her plea at the Zurich congress. Although the delegates came from 16 different nations, they thought alike on issues of peace. The congress immediately passed a resolution calling for an end to the food blockade against the Central Powers. The resolution was telegraphed to Paris, where world leaders were working on the terms of a final peace treaty.

A short time later, Jane addressed the congress. She announced that President Wilson had replied to their telegram. "Your message appeals both to my head and my heart," declared the president. However, the outlook for ending the blockade, he said, "is extremely unpromising."

When delegates received an advance copy of the Treaty of Versailles, which officially ended the war, they understood why. The Allied leaders wanted to punish the Central Powers, especially Germany. The women immediately drafted a series of resolutions responding to the treaty. They charged that a hate-filled document planted the seeds for a future war.

They asked Allied leaders to embrace the Fourteen Points—the peace plan proposed by President Wilson.

When the congress ended, the delegates voted to form a permanent organization called the Women's International League for Peace and Freedom (WIL). They elected Jane Addams as president and asked her to carry the Zurich resolutions to President Wilson at the Paris Peace Conference.

In her closing speech, Jane urged the women to believe in their ability to change the world. She proclaimed:

> *We shall have to . . . put a new sort of force into the world and believe that it is . . . the only thing, in this moment of sorrow and death and destruction, that will heal the world and bring it back into a normal condition.*

"People of Good Will"

Jane delivered the resolutions but never got to see the president in person. She did meet with a group of English and American Quakers on a relief mission to Germany. They asked Jane to help them tell the world about the misery of starving German children. Jane called on her friend Herbert Hoover, who also was in Paris. "Germany needs not only food," he said, "she needs people of good will to bring her back to normal relations with the rest of the world." With a response like that, Jane had no choice but to go, and she asked Alice Hamilton to join her

Fourteen Points:

A peace program proposed by President Woodrow Wilson intended to prevent future wars. The program included many of the resolutions first proposed by the Women's Peace Party.

The founders of the Women's International League for Peace and Freedom. Jane is fourth from the left in the front row.

Hungry children line up for food in Europe after World War I.

Communism:

Ownership of all goods and services by the central government, which decides how to distribute everything to its citizens.

Bolsheviks:

A group of revolutionaries who overthrew the Russian czar in 1917 and brought Communism to Russia.

The two women already had seen suffering, but nothing prepared them for what they found in Germany. In food lines everywhere, children stood on pencil-thin legs. Their shoulder blades poked through their clothes like wings. When it was time for the midday meal, most children received a bowl of "war soup," composed of hot water, flour, dried vegetables, and sawdust.

Jane made up her mind to help these innocent victims of war. She was sure that it would be impossible for Americans to deny food to starving children. She was wrong.

"Most Dangerous Woman"

Back home in America, some people were angry that so many Americans had died defending the freedom of others. They protested U.S. involvement in the affairs of foreign nations. Jane believed that a threat to the freedom of any group of people was a threat to all people. She was ready to carry this message around the country.

But from 1919 through most of the 1920s, many Americans tried to silence Jane. Her requests for money to feed starving German children provoked a great outcry. In one city, she was heckled for 45 minutes before people allowed her to talk.

The attacks against Jane grew louder when she included hungry Russian children in her appeals for food. The Russian Revolution of 1917 had triggered fear that Communism might spread to the United States. Some government officials now searched for Bolsheviks—or "reds," as Communist revolutionaries were called. Caught up in a panic known as the Red Scare, some people suspected that Jane might be a Bolshevik.

Jane received even greater criticism when she spoke out against mistreating people with unpopular political views. She protested the arrests and deportation of hundreds of foreign-born people, many of whom were wrongly accused of spreading revolution.

At a meeting in Chicago, Jane asked the audience: "And what is it these radicals seek?" In answer to her own question, she declared: "It is the right of free speech and free thought; nothing more than is guaranteed under the Constitution." She then cried: "We are trying to suppress something upon which our very country was founded—liberty!"

Jane's speech set off a wave of protest. A leading military magazine called her "the most dangerous woman in America." Many patriotic groups, such as the Daughters of the American Revolution (DAR) and the American Legion, questioned Jane's loyalty to the United States. "I . . . suggest you adopt 'America First' as your motto for the future," thundered one angry man.

The ugly attacks left their marks on Jane. As she admitted to friends, "You know I am really getting old. I find it not as easy to love my enemies as I used to." But she refused to abandon her defense of free speech. She supported the American Civil Liberties Union (ACLU)—formed, as Jane put it, "to contest in the courts all attempts 'to violate the right of free speech, free press, and free assembly.'"

Jane's beliefs cost her dearly. All through the 1920s, her name was recommended for the Nobel Peace Prize—and each time it was turned down. She wrote books, such as *Peace and Bread in Time of War*, but few people bought them. She stopped giving lectures, because few people invited her to speak.

Deportation:

The forcing of an immigrant to return to his or her country of origin, usually for criminal or political reasons.

A portrait of Jane Addams, taken sometime in the 1920s.

ACLU:

A group formed in 1920 to protect the basic rights guaranteed by the Constitution.

Looking to the World

Rejected at home, Jane spent more time traveling abroad. Everywhere she went, people welcomed her warmly. "[I]t seems," remarked Jane, "as if an internationally minded person should be defined as a friend of every country except his own."

As Jane traveled the world, she sensed the coming of another war. She expressed grave concern over "the divided nations of Europe" and the standing armies in more than 50 nations. She worried about the lack of power given to the League of Nations and the refusal of the United States to join.

Jane devoted most of her time to WIL and other peace organizations. She kept up a busy pace, despite surgery on a tumor in 1922 and a heart attack in 1926. Still suffering from a "bad heart," she headed to Honolulu, Hawaii, in 1928. There, she chaired a meeting of the Pan-Pacific Women's Union. The following year, Jane presided over the annual conference of WIL in Prague, Czechoslovakia.

By the end of the Prague conference, however, Jane's poor health made her think she should resign as WIL president. Some delegates could not imagine WIL without Jane. Instead of accepting her resignation, they voted her honorary president for life. At age 69, Jane accepted the title and plunged ahead into a new decade—in the nation's history and in her own life.

League of Nations:

An alliance of nations formed following World War I; its purpose was settling world conflicts by negotiation rather than by military force.

Photo courtesy of Swarthmore College Peace Collection.

Delegates to the Pan-Pacific conference in Honolulu, Hawaii, in 1928. Jane is third from the right in the front row.

A New Decade

In 1929, Hull House turned 40 years old. That same year, the United States entered the Great Depression. As economic hardship gripped the nation, the goal of Hull House—helping the poor—became a priority once more.

In honor of the settlement's 40th anniversary, Jane wrote a new book, *The Second Twenty Years at Hull-House*, describing her experiences since 1909. She also planned a grand reunion for the many settlers and immigrants who had passed through the doors of Hull House.

The three-day celebration took place in June 1930. A movie crew recorded the event. Newspapers reported tributes to Jane. Through the years, Jane had remained the same. She still talked of peace and spoke out against government policies she disliked. The nation had changed, however. Shocked by the Great Depression, people gained a new appreciation of Jane's work with the poor. The word "un-American" no longer seemed to fit the woman who had founded Hull House.

"Another Foot of Progress"

On September 6, 1930, Jane turned 70. Although tired and in poor health, she showed no signs of slowing down. In a birthday interview, she told a reporter:

> *[T]here are new causes, new slogans to work for, new conflicts to be solved and settled, another foot of progress to be made.*

Great Depression:
A major slump in the U.S. economy, triggered in 1929 by a crash of the stock market and resulting in bank failures and massive unemployment.

The front doors of Hull House.

Jane Addams (right) traveled to Washington, D.C., to present a peace petition to the president.

Disarmament:
Voluntarily stopping the production of new military equipment and willingly destroying existing military equipment.

The Nobel Peace Prize presented to Jane Addams.

As the 1930s began, Jane tried to find ways to ease the suffering of the Great Depression. She fought for old-age pensions for the elderly and job opportunities for youth. She also continued to campaign for world peace.

In October 1931, Jane delivered a petition in favor of international disarmament signed by more than 200,000 American women voters. She presented it to her old friend Herbert Hoover, who was now president of the United States. She pledged to deliver millions of other signatures from women overseas.

A month later, Jane became ill with a severe lung infection. Doctors discovered a tumor that had to be removed as soon as the infection cleared. Her nephew James Weber Linn rushed to see his aunt. As Jane lay in her sickbed, she told him: "I have something to tell you, but I'd better not, it's strictly confidential."

"About your operation?" he asked.

Jane smiled and told her nephew that it was "something much nicer."

He begged her to tell him. "Go over to the bureau and open the second drawer on the left," said Jane. "There is a telegram. . . . You can read it, but you must be quiet."

The telegram informed Jane that, along with Dr. Nicholas Butler, she had won the Nobel Peace Prize for 1931. She was the first American woman to win this honor.

Jane's operation kept her from accepting the award in person. Instead, she received telegrams from all over the world. She also received $16,480 in prize money, which she donated to the two great causes in her life—the Women's International League for Peace and Freedom and her unemployed neighbors around Hull House.

Final Battles

Jane never fully recovered from her operation, but she kept on working. In 1934, one of her young relatives asked Jane, "At what age does one begin to feel that he is over that famous crest, and on that famous downhill slope of life?"

"I don't know," laughed Jane. "Apparently not at seventy-three."

By this time, Jane was caught up in the excitement of Franklin Roosevelt's New Deal. Elected president in 1932, Roosevelt had won Jane's support for his efforts to ease poverty. She delivered radio broadcasts to defend his unemployment programs. She also backed his appointment of Frances Perkins as secretary of labor. Perkins was a former Hull House resident and the first woman cabinet member.

In the spring of 1935, the most active woman in the Roosevelt administration— First Lady Eleanor Roosevelt—invited Jane to the White House. She wanted to honor the Women's International League. At a banquet, Eleanor praised Jane for her innovations in promoting freedom. She called her "a pioneer who was still pioneering." In a personal tribute, Eleanor declared:

> *When the day comes when difficulties are faced and settled without resorting to . . . war, . . . we shall look back . . . upon the leadership you have given us, Miss Addams, and be grateful.*

Eleanor Roosevelt.

Top: Frances Perkins.

New Deal:

Government-backed work programs established by President Franklin Roosevelt during the Great Depression to create jobs for the unemployed, relief for the needy, economic recovery, and financial reform.

Cabinet:

A body of presidential appointees who advise the president and head up the major departments within the government.

Jane Addams (1860-1935), American social settlement worker and peace advocate, at her summer home in Bar Harbor, Maine.

Ten days later, Jane felt a sharp pain in her stomach. On May 18, she was sent to the hospital for an operation. When Jane came out of surgery, she murmured, "I had an old doctor friend who told me that the hardest thing in the world was to kill an old woman. He seems to have been right."

Her friend Alice Hamilton knew that Jane suffered from incurable cancer but decided not to tell her. If Jane guessed the truth about her condition, she never let anyone know.

On Monday morning, May 21, 1935, the news went out to the world. Jane Addams—the woman who had endured hatred in the name of peace—had died. But her innovations for peace and personal freedom would live on.

Final Words

Epilogue

Thousands of people gather in the Hull House courtyard for the funeral of Jane Addams in 1935.

Wallace Kirkland photo courtesy of University of Illinois at Chicago, neg. 520.

$\mathcal{P}$eople stood in long lines for two days to say a final good-bye to Jane Addams—leaving a flower, a prayer, or a written message by her casket. As her six-year-old grandniece waited her turn, she whispered: "Are we all Aunt Jane's children?"

The extended family of Hull House thought so. Jane had invited the world into her home. She had encouraged her guests to take part in a social experiment, believing that humans could work together to solve any problem—poverty, intolerance, or war.

Can one small woman really make a difference by tackling such huge global problems? When the doors of Hull House opened in 1889, social workers did not exist. Today, there are hundreds of thousands of them—working to improve conditions wherever they serve. But Jane did more than invent a new profession. She also inspired people to volunteer their energies to help a city, a country, or the world. She celebrated a United States enriched by the diversity of immigration and global contacts. Instead of fearing this diversity, she embraced it. She believed acceptance of individual differences was the cornerstone of democracy.

Perhaps Jane's greatest accomplishment was her willingness to be an innovator. In words that captured her pioneering spirit, Jane remarked: "Our doubts are traitors and make us lose the good we often might win, by fearing to attempt." Jane's courage has left a lasting legacy in America and the world.

Friends and family of Jane Addams attend her funeral.

Jane Addams, late in her life, enjoying time with one of the children of Hull House.

United States Landmarks for Jane Addams

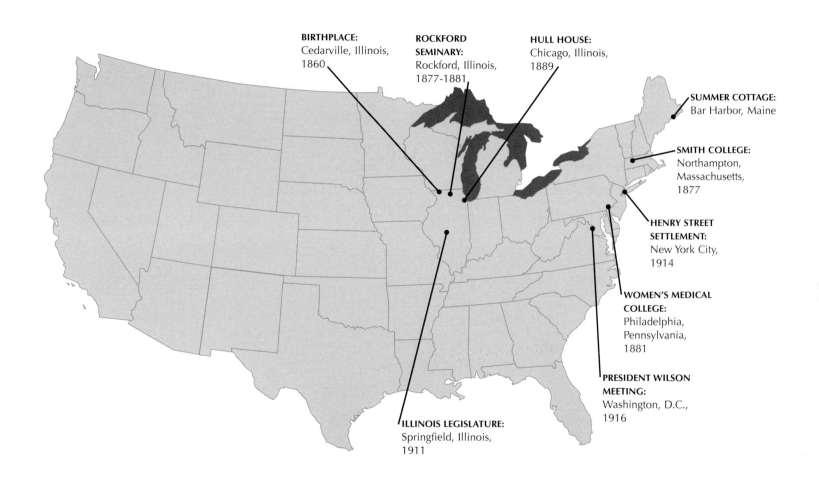

BIRTHPLACE: Cedarville, Illinois, 1860

ROCKFORD SEMINARY: Rockford, Illinois, 1877-1881

HULL HOUSE: Chicago, Illinois, 1889

SUMMER COTTAGE: Bar Harbor, Maine

SMITH COLLEGE: Northampton, Massachusetts, 1877

HENRY STREET SETTLEMENT: New York City, 1914

WOMEN'S MEDICAL COLLEGE: Philadelphia, Pennsylvania, 1881

PRESIDENT WILSON MEETING: Washington, D.C., 1916

ILLINOIS LEGISLATURE: Springfield, Illinois, 1911

The World that Jane Addams Touched

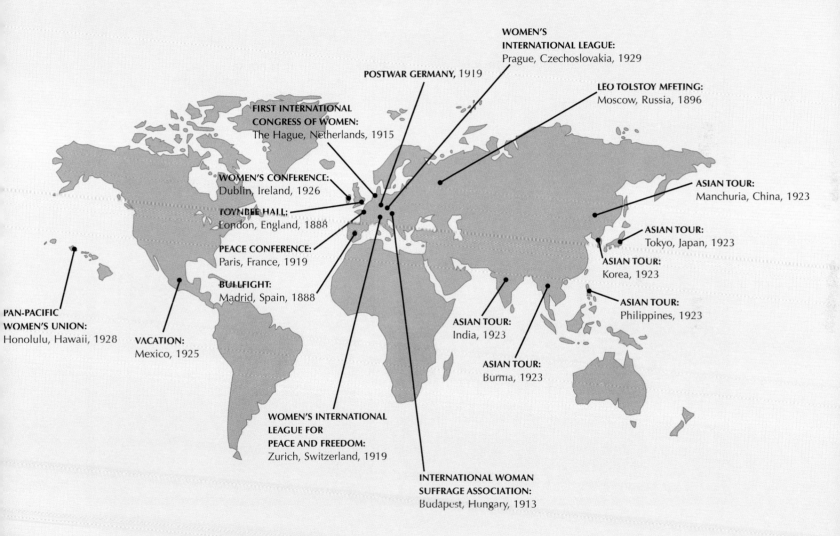

WOMEN'S INTERNATIONAL LEAGUE: Prague, Czechoslovakia, 1929

POSTWAR GERMANY, 1919

LEO TOLSTOY MEETING: Moscow, Russia, 1896

FIRST INTERNATIONAL CONGRESS OF WOMEN: The Hague, Netherlands, 1915

WOMEN'S CONFERENCE: Dublin, Ireland, 1926

ASIAN TOUR: Manchuria, China, 1923

TOYNBEE HALL: London, England, 1888

ASIAN TOUR: Tokyo, Japan, 1923

PEACE CONFERENCE: Paris, France, 1919

ASIAN TOUR: Korea, 1923

BULLFIGHT: Madrid, Spain, 1888

ASIAN TOUR: Philippines, 1923

PAN-PACIFIC WOMEN'S UNION: Honolulu, Hawaii, 1928

VACATION: Mexico, 1925

ASIAN TOUR: India, 1923

ASIAN TOUR: Burma, 1923

WOMEN'S INTERNATIONAL LEAGUE FOR PEACE AND FREEDOM: Zurich, Switzerland, 1919

INTERNATIONAL WOMAN SUFFRAGE ASSOCIATION: Budapest, Hungary, 1913

Hull House, Chicago, Illinois.

Drawing courtesy of University of Illinois at Chicago, neg. 917.

A House Stands on a Busy Street
The Commons, April 1905
By Jane Addams

A house stands on a busy street,
    Its doors are opened wide,
To all who come it bids "Good cheer,"
    To some it says: "Abide."
Gathered within its friendly walls
    A club of women find
The joys of glad companionship,
    Contentment for the mind.

For they have learned what all must learn,
    That in life's hardest storm
The shelter we together build
    Is all that keeps us warm;
That fellowship is heaven-sent
    That it alone can free
The human heart from bitterness,
    And give it liberty.

Some hours they spend in quiet mood,
    On poet's wings up-borne,
They lose themselves in other's joys
    Or weep with those who mourn.

Some hours by traveled mem'ry led
    To foreign lands they roam;
Some hours they bide beside the hearth
    And talk of things of home.

Some hours they sit 'neath music's spell,
    And when the air is rife
With all the magic of sweet sound,
    It heals the pang of life.
Some hours they dream with civic pride
    Of cities that shall be,
Within those streets each citizen,
    Shall live life worthily.

Some hours they sew with tender thought,
    To keep one mem'ry green;
They talk of those whose lives are hard,
    Who suffer wrongs unseen.
They ever open wide their hearts
    To all who are oppressed,
And in life's strange perplexities
    They strive for what is best.

Acknowledgments

The editors wish to thank the following individuals and organizations for their valuable assistance in the preparation of this book:

The staff of the Prints and Photographs Division of the Library of Congress, Washington, D.C.

The staff of the National Archives, Washington, D.C.

The Chicago Historical Society

The staff of the Jane Addams Memorial Collection, University Library, University of Illinois at Chicago

Wendy Chmielewski and her staff at the Swarthmore College Library Peace Collection

Vassar College, for use of original publications and references related to the Jane Addams papers

Mary Ann Johnson at the Hull House Museum for her early support of our research efforts

Paul Fuqua, for photo research and contacts at the Hull House Museum

Additional Photo Credits

Cover, *Wallace Kirkland photo courtesy of University of Illinois at Chicago, neg. 494.*

End papers, *Photo courtesy of University of Illinois at Chicago, neg. 1003.*

page 4, *Photo courtesy of University of Illinois at Chicago, neg. 1146.*

page 15, *Photo courtesy of Swarthmore College Peace Collection.*

page 16, *Photo courtesy of Library of Congress, LC-USZ62-11191.*

page 25, *Wallace Kirkland photo courtesy of University of Illinois at Chicago, neg. 796.*

page 26, *Photo courtesy of Library of Congress.*

page 35, *Photo courtesy of University of Illinois at Chicago, neg. 848.*

page 36, *Photo courtesy of University of Illinois at Chicago, neg. 992.*

page 48, *Photo courtesy of Library of Congress, LC-USZ62-11203.*

page 61, *Wallace Kirkland photo courtesy of University of Illinois at Chicago, neg. 1252.*

page 62, *Photo courtesy of University of Illinois at Chicago, neg. 620.*

page 73, *Photo courtesy of Library of Congress, LC-USZ62-31799.*

page 74, *Photo courtesy of Chicago Historical Society, ICHi-01993.*

page 87, *Photo courtesy of University of Illinois at Chicago, neg. 64.*

page 88, *Photo courtesy of National Archives, 111-SC-94980.*

page 96, *Wallace Kirkland photo courtesy of University of Illinois at Chicago, neg. 54.*

page 97, *Photo courtesy of Franklin D. Roosevelt Library, NPX 71-67.*

page 109, *Photo courtesy of CORBIS/Bettmann, BE037468.*

Bibliography

Addams, Jane. "Patriotism and Pacifists in War Time," *City Club Bulletin*, Vol. X, No. 9, June 16, 1917.

————. *Peace and Bread in Time of War*. New York: King's Crown Press, 1945.

————. *The Second Twenty Years at Hull-House*. New York: Macmillan, 1930.

————. *Twenty Years at Hull-House*. New York: Macmillan, 1910.

————. *Twenty Years at Hull-House, with Autobiographical Notes*. Chicago: University of Illinois Press, 1990.

————. *Women at The Hague*. New York: Macmillan, 1915.

Anticaglia, Elizabeth. "Jane Addams," in *12 American Women*. Chicago: Nelson-Hall, 1980.

Bryan, Mary Lynn McCree, and Allen F. Davis. *100 Years at Hull-House*. Bloomington: Indiana University Press, 1990.

Cook, Blanche Wiesen. *Eleanor Roosevelt, Vol. 1: 1884-1933*. New York: Penguin Books, 1992.

Davis, Allen F. *American Heroine: The Life and Legend of Jane Addams*. New York: Oxford University Press, 1973.

Davis, Allen F., and Mary Lynn McCree. *Eighty Years at Hull-House*. Chicago: Quadrangle Books, 1969.

Deegan, Mary Jo. *Jane Addams and the Men of the Chicago School, 1892-1918*. New Brunswick, N.J.: Transaction, 1988.

Farrell, John C. *Beloved Lady: A History of Jane Addams' Ideas on Reform and Peace*. Baltimore: Johns Hopkins Press, 1967.

Hull-House Maps and Papers. New York: Thomas Y. Crowell, 1895.

Jane Addams: A Centennial Reader. New York: Macmillan, 1960.

Johnson, Mary Ann. *The Many Faces of Hull-House: The Photographs of Wallace Kirkland*. Chicago: University of Illinois Press, 1989.

Lash, Christopher, ed. *The Social Thought of Jane Addams*. Indianapolis: Bobbs-Merrill, 1965.

Levine, Daniel. *Jane Addams and the Liberal Tradition*. Madison: State Historical Society of Wisconsin, 1971.

Linn, James Weber. *Jane Addams: A Biography*. New York: D. Appleton-Century, 1935.

Mowry, George E. *The Era of Theodore Roosevelt and the Birth of Modern America, 1900-1912*. New York: Harper and Row, 1958.

Oakley, Violet. *Cathedral of Compassion: Dramatic Outline of the Life of Jane Addams, 1860-1935*. The Hague, Netherlands: Women's International League for Peace and Freedom, 1955.

Smith, Page. *America Enters the World: A People's History of the Progressive Era and World War I*. New York: McGraw-Hill, 1985.

Wertheimer, Barbara Mayer. *We Were There: The Story of Working Women in America*. New York: Pantheon Books, 1977.

Woloch, Nancy. *Women and the American Experience*. New York: Alfred A. Knopf, 1984.

Sources for Quotations

The following sources provided the quotations in this book:

Prologue

"We find that the contractor bid"

Levine, *Jane Addams and the Liberal Tradition*, p. 74

"How fetching she would look"

Davis, *American Heroine*, p. 121

Chapter 1

"To my amazement"

Addams, *Twenty Years at Hull-House*, p. 15

"I imagined him . . . reading"

Addams, *Twenty Years at Hull-House*, p. 8

"I declared with much firmness"

Addams, *Twenty Years at Hull-House*, p. 5

"[I received] the reply that"

Addams, *Twenty Years at Hull-House*, p. 9

Chapter 2

"The opportunity for our"

Addams, *Twenty Years at Hull-House*, p. 33

"We never speculated as to why"

Linn, *Jane Addams: A Biography*, p. 47

"Woman has gained a new confidence"

Farrell, *Beloved Lady*, p. 36

"I have never since been able to see"

Addams, *Twenty Years at Hull-House*, p. 42

Chapter 3

"[A]bout two hundred children"

Farrell, *Beloved Lady*, p. 56

"a fine old house"

Addams, *Twenty Years at Hull-House*, p. 56

"[I]t seemed understood that we"

Addams, *Twenty Years at Hull-House*, p. 65

"Our young people hear in every sermon"

Davis, *American Heroine*, p. 65

Chapter 4

"Sure, Mary, you must go"

Davis and McCree, *Eighty Years at Hull-House*, p. 34

"I remember a little girl of four"

Addams, *Twenty Years at Hull-House*, p. 118

"The organization of society"

Hull-House Maps and Papers, p. 199

Chapter 5

"Hull-House . . . perceived that"

Davis and McCree, *Eighty Years at Hull-House*, p. 74

"One function of the settlement"
  Woloch, *Women and the American Experience*, p. 262

Chapter 6
"The Progressive Party, believing"
  Davis, *American Heroine*, p. 188
"Some of us are very much disturbed"
  Levine, *Jane Addams and the Liberal Tradition*, p. 193
"[W]omen doctors, women lawyers"
  Smith, *America Enters the World*, p. 331
"Not a breath, not a tremor of the future"
  Addams, *The Second Twenty Years at Hull-House*, p. 81
"All of us, through long experiences"
  Addams, *Peace and Bread in Time of War*, p. 3
"We, [the] women of the United States"
  Davis, *American Heroine*, p. 216

Chapter 7
"Generally speaking, we heard everywhere"
  Davis, *American Heroine*, p. 216

"Miss Addams denies him the credit"
  Davis, *American Heroine*, p. 227
"If Jane Addams is a careful reader"
  Davis, *American Heroine*, p. 230
"[I]t was at this time that I first learned"
  Addams, *The Second Twenty Years at Hull-House*, p. 133
"It seemed at last, as if peace were assured"
  Addams, *Peace and Bread in Time of War*, p. 58
"What I am opposed to is not"
  Smith, *America Enters the World*, p. 515
"All that had been told them"
  Addams, *Peace and Bread in Time of War*, p. 118

Chapter 8
"We shall have to"
  Davis, *American Heroine*, p. 259
"[T]here are new causes"
  Levine, *Jane Addams and the Liberal Tradition*, p. 240
"When the day comes"
  Linn, *Jane Addams: A Biography*, p. 415

Index

A

Abolitionist: definition, 67

Absinthe: definition, 89

Accomplishments of Jane Addams, 111, *112-113*

ACLU (American Civil Liberties Union): definition, 103

Addams, Anna Haldeman (stepmother), 22-24, *24, 30,* 32

Addams house in Cedarville (Illinois), *19, 22*

Addams, Jane, *10, 14, 57, 69, 71-72, 75, 80, 82, 86, 89, 91, 92, 100-101, 103, 104, 106, 108, 111;* as a child, *17-18, 21; maps* 112, 113; quoted, 11, 17, 19, 21, 28, 29, 32, 40, 41, 43, 45, 54, 56, 65, 76, 79, 81, 89, 91, 92, 95, 101, 105; as a young woman, *12, 24, 27, 29, 32, 37*

Addams, John Huy (father), 14, 17-22, *21, 24, 30;* death of, 30; lumber and flour mills owned by, *20, 23;* remarriage to Anna Haldeman, 22-24

Addams, John Weber (brother), *31*

Addams, Sarah Alice (sister), *31*

Addams, Sarah Weber (mother), *18,* 19; death of, 17-18

AFL (American Federation of Labor): definition, 54

African Americans: famous leaders, *68;* NAACP, 68; prejudice against, 67-68; settlement houses for migrants, 67

Alderman: definition, 13

Alliances: definition, 79

Amendment: definition, 69

American Civil Liberties Union (ACLU): definition, 103

American Federation of Labor (AFL): definition, 54

Americanized: definition, 64

American Union Against Militarism, 81

Anarchists: definition, 40; Addams' experience of, 40-41, 65-66; and McKinley shooting, 65-66

Apartment building for working women, 51-52

Appendix: definition, 30

B

Bachelor's degrees for women, *28*

Backlash: definition, 55

Base: definition, 86

Belgium, food distribution to, 95-96

Blacklisted: definition, 56

Blockade: definition, 100

Boarding club for women workers, 51-52

Bolsheviks: definition, 102

Bombing of police in Haymarket riot, *40*

Bookbinding: definition, 49

Books by Jane Addams, 55, 71, 103, 105

Boss: definition, 13

Bowen, Louise deKoven, 51, 58

Bullfight in Spain, *33*

Burglaries at Hull House, 43

Butcher shop in Hull House neighborhood, 55

C

Cabinet: definition, 107

Cablegram: definition, 82

Capital: definition, 56

Carter, Orrin, 94

Cartoons: Progressive Party, *76;* Wilson's World War I policy, *93*

Catt, Carrie Chapman, *81*

Architectural plans of Hull House, *60*

Argonne region in France (World War I), *99*

Assassination: definition, 17; of Abraham Lincoln, *17;* of Archduke Francis Ferdinand, 79-80

Auction of decayed food in London, 32

Aurora (Missouri) parade supporting World War I, *94*

Averbuch, police shooting of, 66-67

Cedarville: Addams house, *19, 22;* mills owned by John Addams, *20, 23*

Central Powers, food blockades against, 100-101

Chicago: butcher shop in Hull House neighborhood, *55;* children outside apartment building, *67;* children playing in alley, *9;* children playing on garbage bin, *11;* Haymarket riot, *40;* health code violations by trash, 10-11; horse-drawn garbage wagon, *12;* immigrant children, *8, 56, 63;* immigrant population, 39-40; police arrests, *13,* 66; political corruption in, 13-14; poor neighborhood, around 1900, *38;* tenement districts, *39, 45. See also* Hull House

Childhood (of Addams), 17-24, *17-18, 21;* Cedarville house, *19, 22;* physical problems, 21; stepbrother, 23; stepmother, 22-24

Child labor, 53-54, *75*

Children: child labor, 53-54, *75;* cooking class at Hull House, *63;* exercise class at Hull House, *53;* gaps between immigrant parents and Americanized children, 63-64; immigrant children, *8, 56, 63;* juvenile courts, 58; nursery at Hull House, *45;* outside apartment building, *67;* playground at Hull House, 52-53; playing in alley, *9;* playing on garbage bin, *11;* starvation in Europe and Russia, 95-96, 100-102, *102*

Church as hospital in World War I, *90*

Churches: support of Hull House, 38-39

Citizenship: citizenship class at Hull House, *95;* and military draft, 95

Civil-rights movement: definition, 68

Classes at Hull House: citizenship class, *95;* cooking class, *63;* exercise class, *53;* Labor Museum, 63-64

Clothing: homespun, 63; knickerbockers, 12

College education of Jane Addams: medical studies, 30; Rockford Female Seminary, 27-30, *27, 29;* Smith entrance exam, 27

Colleges for women, *28*

burglaries, 43; citizenship class, *95;* cooking class, *63;* exercise class, *53;* front doors, *105;* fundraising for, 37-39; funeral of Jane Addams, *110-111;* ghost in, 40-41; in the Great Depression, 105; history of, 42; Labor Museum, *63-64;* neighborhood, 41-42, 43-45, 55; neighbors, *11, 44, 55, 56;* nursery, *45;* playground, 52-*53;* poem about, 115; police arresting man near, *13;* publicity for, 38-39; residents, *50-52, 99;* reunion, 105; visitors, *43, 46;* wool spinning, *64*
Hull-House Maps and Papers (Addams), 55

I

Illnesses: filth diseases, 9; trash as cause, 9-10, 57; typhoid fever, 13. *See also* Illness of Jane Addams
Illness of Jane Addams, 13, 91, 104, 106, 108; spinal curvature, 21, 31
Immigrant children, *8, 56, 63*
Immigrants: definition, 9; arriving in the United States, *63;* in Chicago, 39-40, 56; children, *8, 56, 63;* citizenship class at Hull House, *95;* cooking class at Hull House, *63;* cultures and crafts of, 63-64; gaps between parents and Americanized children, 63-64; at Hull House, *43;* Italian women and their children, *44, 63;* prejudice toward, 64-68; Russian immigrant family, *65*
Indifference: definition, 33
Inequality: definition, 22; beginning of concern about, 21-22. *See also* Poverty
Inheritance of Jane Addams, 31
Installment plan: definition, 42
International women's peace congress, 82-86, *83*
Isaak, Abraham, 65-66
Italian women and their children, *44, 63*

J

Jacobs, Alleta, 82
"Jane Club," 51-52
Jews: prejudice against, 65-67
Jobs: garbage inspector job, 11-13, 14
Justice system: injustices toward immigrants, 65-67; juvenile courts, 58, 67
Juvenile court campaign, *58,* 67
Juvenile delinquents: definition, 58

K

Kelley, Florence, 50-*51,* 53-54, 55
Kenney, Mary, *49*-50, 51
Kent, William, 52-53
Key events in Jane Addams' life, 4, 16, 26, 36, 48, 62, 74, 88, 98; *maps* 112, 113
Knickerbockers: definition, 12

L

Labor Museum, 63-64
Labor organization, 49-50, 51, 53-57, *54,* 75; labor meeting, *54. See also* Factories; Strike
Landmarks for Jane Addams: *map* 112
Lathrop, Julia, *50,* 51, 58, *92*
League of Nations: definition, 104
Legal system: injustices toward immigrants, 65-67; juvenile courts, 58, 67
Life experiences: *maps* 112, 113
Lincoln, Abraham, *19;* assassination of, *17*
Linn, John (nephew), *99*
Linn, Stanley R. (nephew), 9-*10,* 57
London: auction of decayed food, 32; homeless people, *32;* Jane's travels to, 32-34; settlement houses, *34*
Lumber and flour mills owned by John Addams, *20, 23*

Lusitania: sinking of, 84, *85*
Lynchings: definition, 67

M

McDowell, Mary, *92*
McKinley, William: shooting of, 65
Mandate: definition, 92
Medical studies, 30
Migrant workers: settlement houses for, 67
Mills owned by John Addams, *20, 23*
Ministers: support of Hull House, 38-39
Missionaries: definition, 27
Moral education, 19-22

N

NAACP (National Association for the Advancement of Colored People), 68
National American Woman Suffrage Association (NAWSA), 69
Nationalist: definition, 79
NAWSA (National American Woman Suffrage Association), 69
Neighborhood of Hull House, 41-42, 43-45, 55
Neighbors of Hull House, *11, 44, 55, 56*
Netherlands: international women's peace congress, 82-86, *83*
Neutrality: definition, 81
New Deal: definition, 107
Newer Ideals of Peace (Addams), 71
19th Amendment: definition, 92
Nobel Peace Prize, 75, 103, *106*
No man's land: definition, 80
Nursery at Hull House, *45*

Time Life Education Inc. is a division of Time Life Inc.

TIME LIFE INC.
PRESIDENT AND CEO: Jim Nelson

TIME LIFE EDUCATION INC.
PRESIDENT: Mary Davis Holt

Time-Life History Makers
JANE ADDAMS: FREEDOM'S INNOVATOR

Managing Editor: Mary J. Wright
Series Editor and Editorial Director: Bonnie H. Hobson

Research and Writing: Deborah A. Parks
Deborah Parks graduated from the State University of New York at Stony Brook.
She completed graduate studies at the City College of New York and Columbia
University. She has taught social studies and history at the middle-school, high-
school, and college levels. She currently works as an editor, writer, and author.

Research Consultant: Ben F. Collins

Text Editor: Phillip J. Berardelli
Picture Research: Joan Marie Mathys
Associate Editor/Research and Writing: Laura Heinle
Picture Associate: Angela Bailey
Editorial Assistant: Maria Washington
Student Researcher: Lindsey George
Technical Art Specialist: John Drummond
Designer: Susan Angrisani, Designsmith, Inc.
Senior Copyeditor: Judith Klein

Prepress service by the Time-Life Imaging Center

Vice President of Marketing and Publisher: Rosalyn McPherson Perkins
Vice President of Book Production: Patricia Pascale
Vice President of Imaging: Marjann Caldwell
Director of Publishing Technology: Betsi McGrath
Director of Photography and Research: John Conrad Weiser
Production Manager: Carolyn Bounds
Director of Quality Assurance: James King
Chief Librarian: Louise D. Forstall

First printing. Printed in U.S.A.

10 9 8 7 6 5 4 3 2 1

School and library distribution by Time-Life Education, P.O. Box 85026,
Richmond, Virginia 23285-5026.
Telephone: 1-800-449-2010
Internet: www.timelifeedu.com

TIME-LIFE is a trademark of Time Warner Inc. and affiliated companies.

Library of Congress Cataloging-in-Publication Data
Parks, Deborah A.
Jane Addams: freedom's innovator
    p.   cm.—(Time-Life history makers)
    Includes bibliographical references and index.
    Summary: Examines the life and times of Jane Addams who, in 1889,
established in Hull House one of the first settlement houses in America and
later became the first American woman to be awarded the Nobel Peace Prize.
    ISBN 0-7835-5445-1
    1. Addams, Jane, 1860-1935—Juvenile literature. 2. Social workers—United
States—Biography—Juvenile literature. 3.Women social workers—United
States—Biography—Juvenile literature. 4. Women social reformers—United
States—Biography—Juvenile literature. 5. Hull House (Chicago, Ill.)—History
—Juvenile literature. 6. Social settlements—Illinois—Chicago—History—
Juvenile literature.[1. Addams, Jane, 1860-1935. 2. Social workers. 3. Women—
Biography. 4. Nobel Prizes—Biography.] I. Title. II. Series.
HV40.32A33 J36   1999
361.92—dc21   99-046876
[b]   CIP

I have never been sure I was right. I have often been doubtful about the next step. We can only fe[el]

I have never been sure I was right. I have often been doubtful about the next step. We can only f[eel]

nature" but we do hope to modify human behavior. . . . Today we cannot get internationalism acros[s]

nature" but we do hope to modify human behavior. . . . Today we cannot get internationalism acr[oss]

men will accept internationalism in the place of separate nationalism, we must be ready with the [

men will accept internationalism in the place of separate nationalism, we must be ready with the

seek to remove the difficulties which arise from each nation seeking to get the most for itself. It w[ould]

seek to remove the difficulties which arise from each nation seeking to get the most for itself. I[t]

relationship. . . . We move slowly, and yet much has occurred in twenty years. If we had said twen[ty]

relationship. . . . We move slowly, and yet much has occurred in twenty years. If we had said tw[enty]

been called idealistic visionaries. . . . Public opinion must come to realize how futile war is. . . . W[

been called idealistic visionaries. . . . Public opinion must come to realize how futile war is. . .

public opinion; moral enterprise. . . . Woodrow Wilson said: "No issue is dead in the world so lo[ng]

public opinion; moral enterprise. . . . Woodrow Wilson said: "No issue is dead in the world so lo[

of statesmanship.

of statesmanship.

Notes from Response by Jane Addams at a Banquet of the Women's International League, 20th Anniversary Celebration, Was[hington]

Notes from Response by Jane Addams at a Banquet of the Women's International League, 20th A[nniversary]